Viva Practice for Intercollegiate MRCS (Part 3)

Christopher L H Chan   **BSc (Hons) MB BS FRCS**
MRC Clinical Fellow in Coloproctology
Academic Department of Surgery
Barts and the London School of Medicine and Dentistry
Whitechapel
London

Alister J Hart   **MA MRCS**
Spr in Orthopaedics and trauma surgery
Barnet General Hospital
London

PASTEST
Dedicated to your success

Egerton Court
Knutsford
Cheshire
WA16 8DX
Telephone: 01565 752000

First edition 2001
Reprinted 2002
Reprinted with updated introduction 2004
Reprinted 2005

ISBN: 1 904627 19 6

A catalogue record for this book is available from the British Library.

PasTest Revision Books and Intensive Courses
PasTest has been established in the field of postgraduate medical education since 1972, providing revision books and intensive study courses for doctors preparing for their professional examinations. Books and courses are available for the following specialties:
MRCS, MRCP Part 1 and Part 2, MRCPCH Part 1 and Part 2, MRCOG, DRCOG, MRCGP, MRCPsych, DCH, FRCA and PLAB.

For further details contact:

PasTest Ltd, Knutsford, Cheshire, WA16 8DX
Tel: 01565 752000   Fax: 01565 650264
Email: enquiries@pastest.co.uk   Web site: www. pastest.co.uk

---

Typeset by Breeze Ltd, Manchester
Printed by Bell and Bain Ltd, Glasgow

Contents

Introduction

This book is intended primarily for candidates sitting the Oral component of the Intercollegiate MRCS examination. The aim of this book is to provide a framework for candidates to practise answering viva questions, to help prepare for the different sections of the examination.

This book covers the most popular viva topics and specific questions have been included either because they are very commonly asked or cover a particular part of the syllabus that is easily missed during revision.

Answering questions in the Oral component of the exam is stressful but it is important to formulate and convey your knowledge to the examiner. To do this successfully, we believe that all answers should adhere to three main principles:
* The answer should be structured
* The key elements and points should be emphasized and discussed first
* The language should be concise and succinct

If these principles are followed, the candidate will demonstrate a clear, logical approach and a good answer would be presented.

The answers provided in this book are detailed and in some instances provide more information than required. This is primarily to benefit the candidate, by trying to instil greater confidence if he or she should encounter a similar question. Some answers have bold text, this is for ease of reading and to aid revision.

The design of this book is modelled on the format of the Oral component of the exam itself. Hence there are three main sections in the book, corresponding to the three sections of the Oral component of the Part 3 MRCS exam:
1. **Applied surgical anatomy and operative surgery**
2. **Clinical pathology and principles of surgery**
3. **Applied physiology and critical care**

Each section of the book is further sub-divided into subject areas.

Each oral lasts for 20 minutes and consists of two 10 minute vivas from a pair of examiners. On average, candidates cover three subject areas in each 10 minute viva. The depth to the questioning is dependent on the candidate's knowledge and ability. Hence, good candidates are questioned in greater depth until they are unable to answer correctly. Equally, candidates who are poor in one particular subject area are questioned on at least two other subject areas.

This book should help you focus your revision and allow you to test your ability and verbalise your knowledge. We make no apology for the orientation of the questions towards the Basic Sciences, as this is an accurate reflection of the exam.

Do remember that the examiner is trying to pass you. The examiner will need evidence to pass you but do not become despondent if you occasionally answer incorrectly, particularly if you have covered many different topics. We hope that this book will enhance your chances of success in the examination.

Good luck!

Regulations for Oral Component

- The Oral is the first component of Part 3 of the MRCS, the other component is the clinical

- Candidates must pass the Oral component in order to proceed to the clinical component

- The Oral section of the Intercollegiate MRCS examination will be conducted up to three times a year at The Royal College of Surgeons of England

- Candidates must pass both Part 1 and Part 2 before proceeding to the Oral section of the exam

- The questions in the Oral section will cover the whole syllabus

- The Oral section will consist of three vivas, each lasting 20 minutes in

  - Applied surgical anatomy and operative surgery
  - Clinical pathology and principles of surgery
  - Applied physiology and critical care

- Candidates will be awarded a 'pass' or 'fail'

APPLIED SURGICAL ANATOMY AND OPERATIVE SURGERY

1.   First rib
2.   Mastoid antrum
3.   Meninges and dural venous sinuses
4.   Skull foramina
5.   Circle of Willis and cerebral blood supply
6.   Cavernous sinus
7.   Thyroid gland
8.   Submandibular gland
9.   The root of the neck
10.   Diaphragm
11.   Parotid gland
12.   Pancreas and spleen
13.   Vascular supply of the large bowel
14.   Femoral triangle
15.   Vertebrae and the vertebral column
16.   Arterial supply of the lower limb
17.   The breast
18.   Coronary arteries
19.   Axillary node sampling
20.   Lumbar vertebrae
21.   Transpyloric plane of Addison
22.   Shoulder joint and arm
23.   Radial nerve
24.   Median nerve
25.   Forearm anatomy
26.   Wrist joint
27.   Sciatic nerve and the hip joint
28.   Knee joint
29.   Structures around the medial malleolus
30.   Dermatomes of the lower limb
31.   Carpal tunnel decompression
32.   Right hemicolectomy
33.   Pneumoperitoneum
34.   Femoral hernia repair
35.   Positioning of the surgical patient
36.   Surgical diathermy
37.   Appendicectomy
38.   Laparoscopic cholecystectomy
39.   Emergency tracheostomy
40.   Tonsillectomy

1.   FIRST RIB

How many tubercles are there on the first rib?

Two.

Where are these tubercles situated?

The tubercle of the first rib forms the most posterior convexity of the rib and is found at the junction of the neck and shaft. The other tubercle called the scalene tubercle is a ridge found on the superior surface of the shaft of the rib, in between the grooves for the subclavian artery and vein.

What runs in the subclavian grooves?

The **lower trunk of the brachial plexus** (anterior rami of T1 and C8) runs in the groove behind the scalene tubercle. This groove is called the groove for the subclavian artery but the artery does not actually lie in it. The subclavian artery is only in contact with the outer border of the rib. The **subclavian vein** runs in the groove anterior to the scalene tubercle.

What attaches to the scalene tubercle?

Scalenus anterior.

Which part of the subclavian artery lies behind scalenus anterior?

The second part of the subclavian artery.

What important structures lie in front of the neck of the first rib?

From medial to lateral: the **stellate ganglion**, the **superior intercostal artery** and the **first thoracic nerve**.

What is the stellate ganglion?

The stellate or cervico-thoracic ganglion is the fusion of the inferior cervical ganglion and first thoracic sympathetic ganglion.

How many facets are present on the head of the first rib?

One.

What does the head of the first rib articulate with?

The head of the first rib articulates with the upper part of the body of the first thoracic vertebra.

2.   MASTOID ANTRUM

In which part of the skull does the mastoid antrum lie?

Posterior part of the petrous temporal bone.

How do the mastoid air cells form during development?

Mastoid air cells arise during the first year of life as tympanic antral diverticula. These air cells burrow out into the thin plates of bone at the bottom of the sigmoid sinus.

They are lined with adherent mucoperiosteum and pneumatise the mastoid process. Occasionally, they may extend into the squamous part of the temporal bone.

How is the mastoid antrum connected to the middle ear?

The mastoid antrum is connected to the epitympanic recess of the middle ear by the aditus.

Why is this connection important?

It is important for two reasons. Firstly, the aditus is a **communication between the middle ear and mastoid air cells** and may act as a portal for infection to spread. Secondly, it is **closely related to the sigmoid sinus and cerebellum**. Thus, a spreading infection can involve these veins (posterior, auricular, mastoid emissary and sigmoid sinus) leading to thrombosis, meningitis, cerebellar or cerebral abscesses.

What is the lymphatic drainage of this region?

The lymph drains to the **mastoid** and **upper deep cervical** lymph nodes.

3. MENINGES AND DURAL VENOUS SINUSES

What are the meninges?

The meninges are three closely apposed tissue layers.

- The **pia mater** covers the surface of the brain and spinal cord.
- The **dura mater** lines the cranial vault and spinal canal. Between the pia and dural mater is the arachnoid mater.
- The **arachnoid mater** is attached to the pia mater by numerous filamentous processes; between these two layers is the subarachnoid space, which is filled with cerebrospinal fluid.

What are the folds of the dura mater?

There are four folds of the dura mater that project into the cranial vault. They all comprise of an inner layer of the dura mater.

- The **tentorium cerebelli** projects from the margins of the transverse sinus and superior petrosal sinuses. The tentorium cerebelli is attached to the posterior clinoid processes, the upper border of the petrous and temporal bones, and the inner surface of the skull to the internal occipital protuberance. The free margin is U-shaped between the anterior clinoid processes, and provides an orifice for the brain stem.
- The **falx cerebri** lies in the midline between the two cerebral hemispheres. It is attached anteriorly to the crista galli of the ethmoid bone and posteriorly to the upper surface of the tentorium cerebelli.
- The **falx cerebelli** projects into the sulcus between the cerebellar hemispheres from the internal occipital protuberance to the posterior margin of the foramen magnum.
- The **diaphragm sellae** forms the roof of the pituitary fossa. It is a horizontal sheet attached to the middle and posterior clinoid processes on both sides. It has an opening to allow passage of the pituitary stalk.

What purpose do these dural folds serve?

The dural folds are thought to minimise rotatory displacement of the brain.

What are the venous sinuses?

The venous sinuses are **large low pressure** veins that lie between the inner and outer layers of the dura except for inferior sagittal and straight sinuses which are between two layers of fibrous dura. These venous sinuses receive blood from the brain and skull and communicate with veins of the scalp and face (emissary veins).

Can you briefly describe the anatomy of the main dural venous sinuses?

- The **superior sagittal sinus** runs in the upper margin of the falx cerebri with the lower sagittal sinus running in its free edge.
- The superior sagittal sinus usually drains to the right to become the **transverse sinus**. The transverse sinus turns inferiorly and becomes the sigmoid sinus and continues as the internal jugular vein at the jugular foramen.
- The **inferior sagittal sinus** runs in the lower free edge of the falx cerebri and posteriorly it joins the great cerebral vein to become the straight sinus.
- The **straight sinus** lies between the folds of the fibrous dura at the junction of the falx cerebri and tentorium cerebelli. It receives the inferior sagittal sinus, right and left basal cerebral veins and single great vein of Galen. It ends at the occipital protuberance by turning into the transverse sinus.

What are the arachnoid villi?

The arachnoid villi are herniations of arachnoid mater projecting into the venous sinuses.

What are the arachnoid granulations?

Arachnoid granulations are villi that are aggregated into visible clumps along the course of the superior sagittal sinus.

What is the function of the arachnoid villi?

Their function is to transport cerebrospinal fluid back into the intra-vascular compartment.

4.   SKULL FORAMINA

What runs through the optic canal?
- Optic nerve (II)
- Dural sheath
- Ophthalmic artery

What runs through the superior orbital fissure?
- Ophthalmic branch of the trigeminal nerve (Va)
- Oculomotor nerve (III) (both superior and inferior divisions)
- Trochlear nerve (IV)
- Abducent nerve (VI)
- Sympathetic fibres
- Ophthalmic veins
- Branches of the middle meningeal and lacrimal arteries

What runs through the foramen magnum?
- Medulla
- Anterior spinal artery (formed from both vertebral arteries)
- Vertebral arteries
- Spinal branches of the accessory (XI) nerve
- Meninges
- Apical ligament of the dens
- Tectorial membrane

What runs through the foramen ovale?
- Mandibular branch of the trigeminal nerve (Vc)
- Lesser petrosal nerve
- Accessory meningeal artery

In which cranial fossa does the facial nerve exit the skull?

The posterior cranial fossa.

Can you briefly describe the optic pathway?

Light is sensed by photoreceptors which synapse with bipolar cells which in turn synapse with retinal ganglion cells. Axons of the retinal ganglion cells pass through optic canal (as optic nerves) in the temporal bone to enter the middle cranial fossa. Nasal retinal fibres decussate to form the optic chiasm and together with the temporal retinal fibres and form the optic tracts. Axons then pass to the lateral geniculate body in the thalamus, synapse and pass to the visual cortex (medial aspect of the occipital lobe).

NB. Some fibres pass to the Edinger-Westphal nucleus in the midbrain instead of the lateral geniculate body. These are responsible for the light reflex and consequent pupil constriction via the parasympathetic fibres carried by the III cranial nerve.

5.   CIRCLE OF WILLIS AND CEREBRAL BLOOD SUPPLY

Can you briefly describe the blood supply to the brain?

Blood is supplied to the brain via two systems: the **internal carotid** (anterior circulation) and the **vertebral** (posterior circulation) **systems**. These arterial systems lie in the subarachnoid space before penetrating the brain substance. Most of the blood is directed towards the grey matter of the cerebral hemispheres.

The internal carotid and vertebral systems anastomose with each other around the optic chiasma to form the **circle of Willis**.

The internal carotid arteries arise from the common carotid arteries which in turn arise from the brachiocephalic trunk on the right and the arch of the aorta on the left. The internal carotid arteries enter the skull through the carotid canal, making five 90° turns before terminating into anterior and middle cerebral branches (part of the circle of Willis) on the medial surface of the temporal lobe.

The two vertebral arteries arise from the first part of the subclavian artery on the corresponding side, having ascended through the foramina of the transverse processes of C6 to C1, accompanied by sympathetic nerves and vertebral veins. The vertebral arteries enter the skull through the foramen magnum and terminate by joining its counterpart at the lower pons to form the basilar artery. The basilar artery ascends between the brain stem and clivus and terminates at the upper border of the pons, to form the two posterior cerebral arteries, thus forming the circle of Willis.

What is the blood supply to the cerebral hemispheres?

The blood supply to the cerebral hemispheres is derived from three cerebral arteries: **anterior**, **middle** and **posterior**.

The **anterior cerebral artery** passes forward above the optic nerve. It is connected to its fellow by the **anterior communicating artery**. The anterior cerebral artery supplies the orbital surface of the frontal lobe and the medial surface of the hemisphere as far back as the parieto-occipital sulcus. It extends onto the superior surface of the hemisphere to anastomose with the middle cerebral artery. Thus, it supplies the part of the cortex that is responsible for motor and sensory areas of the opposite leg.

The **middle cerebral artery** is the largest and most direct branch of the internal carotid artery. It enters the lateral sulcus and radiates over a large area of the cortex, supplying part of the cortex responsible for auditory, speech, motor and sensory control of the contra-lateral half of the body (except the lower limb).

The **posterior cerebral artery** passes backwards above the tentorium to supply the infero-medial surface of the temporal and occipital lobes.

Which of the three arteries is most commonly affected by thromboembolism?

The middle cerebral artery.

Why do you sometimes observe macular sparing in cerebrovascular accidents affecting the posterior cerebral artery territory?

The macula receives a blood supply from the middle cerebral artery as well as the posterior cerebral artery, thus macular sparing is seen.

What is the blood brain barrier?

The blood brain barrier (BBB) is formed by the endothelial cells of the cerebral capillaries. In parts of the body i.e. outside the brain, the walls of the capillaries contain penetrable gaps. However, the brain capillaries are unique in that they have specialised tight junctions between the endothelial cells and a thick basement membrane.

What is the function of the blood brain barrier?

The function of the BBB is to act as a selectively permeable barrier (e.g. permeable to amino acids, amines and sugars) and protect the internal environment of the brain.

6. CAVERNOUS SINUS

What is the cavernous sinus?

It is a dural venous sinus.

How does the cavernous sinus differ from other dural venous sinuses?

The cavernous sinus differs from the other venous sinuses in that it is intersected with septo-fibrous tissue, which divides the blood space into a series of tiny caves.

Where is the cavernous sinus?

The cavernous sinus is found alongside the body of the sphenoid bone in the middle cranial fossa. It lies in the space between the periosteal body of the sphenoid and the fold of fibrous dura.

What lies in the cavity of the cavernous sinus?

The internal carotid artery and the VI cranial nerve lie within the cavernous sinus.

What structures are found within the lateral wall of the cavernous sinus?

The III and IV cranial nerves, ophthalmic and maxillary branches of the V cranial nerve lie within the lateral wall of the cavernous sinus.

What is the relation between the cavernous sinus and the pituitary fossa?

The pituitary fossa lies medial to the cavernous sinus and is separated by a fibrous fold of dura.

7.   THYROID GLAND

Can you describe the immediate anatomical relations of the thyroid?

The thyroid gland is enclosed by pre-tracheal fascia.

- **Posterior** to the isthmus lie the 2nd, 3rd and 4th tracheal rings. Behind the lateral lobes of the thyroid are the parathyroid glands and carotid sheath.
- **Anterior** to each lateral lobe are the sternohyoid, sternothyroid and sternocleidomastoid muscles.
- **Medial** to each lateral lobe are the larynx, trachea, pharynx, oesophagus, inferior constrictor muscle of the pharynx, cricothyroid, the external laryngeal and recurrent laryngeal nerves.

Which nerve is in particular danger during thyroid operations?

The recurrent laryngeal nerve is the nerve that is in the greatest danger during thyroid operations.

What is the effect of damaging the recurrent laryngeal nerve?

Damaging this nerve would cause a vocal cord paralysis on that side, and produce a hoarse voice.

Can you describe the important relationships of the recurrent laryngeal nerve?

The recurrent laryngeal nerve passes upwards in the groove between the trachea and the oesophagus to lie immediately behind the cricothyroid joint. It enters the larynx deep to the inferior constrictor of the pharynx. The nerve often divides into two at the level of the upper border of the thyroid isthmus.

The recurrent laryngeal nerve is closely but variably related to the inferior thyroid artery. On the left the nerve usually lies behind the artery and on the right it is either found behind or between the branches of the artery.

Where would you expect to find the external laryngeal nerve?

The external laryngeal nerve lies posterior to the superior thyroid artery, in contact with the inferior constrictor and cricothyroid muscles. (The external laryngeal nerve is unlikely to be damaged if the artery is ligated at the tip of the upper pole.)

What is the effect of damaging this nerve?

Damage to the external laryngeal nerve produces only a slight hoarseness, which can usually be compensated by the opposite cricothyroid muscle.

What is the arterial blood supply to the thyroid?

Three arteries supply the thyroid gland.

- The **superior thyroid artery**, which is a branch of the external carotid, enters the upper pole of each lateral lobe
- The **inferior thyroid artery**, which is a branch of the thyrocervical trunk divides into four or five branches

outside the pre-tracheal fascia and enters the lower pole
- The **thyroid ima artery**, when present, is a branch of the aortic arch or brachiocephalic trunk and enters the lower part of the isthmus

What is the venous drainage of the thyroid?

Venous blood from the thyroid drains via three routes.

- The **superior thyroid vein** drains the upper pole to the internal jugular or facial vein
- The **middle thyroid vein** drains the lateral lobe directly into the internal jugular vein
- The **inferior thyroid veins** drain the isthmus and lower poles to the brachiocephalic vein

Where are the parathyroid glands in relation to the thyroid gland?

The parathyroid glands normally lie behind the lateral lobes of the thyroid gland usually outside the pre-tracheal fascia. 90% of the population has four glands.

- The **superior glands** on each side usually lie at the level of the junction between the upper and middle thirds of the lateral lobe.
- The **inferior glands** usually lie behind the lower pole, in the angle between the inferior thyroid artery and recurrent laryngeal nerve.

8.   SUBMANDIBULAR GLANDS

Where do you find the submandibular gland?

The submandibular gland lies in the digastric triangle below the mandible. Most of the gland is superficial to the mylohyoid muscle but a small part is deep to the mylohyoid having passed around the posterior free border.

What are the important relations of the submandibular gland?

From superficial to deep

- The facial vein and cervical branch of the facial nerve lie superficial to the gland
- The facial artery lies posteriorly and superiorly before passing onto the face
- The hypoglossal nerve, submandibular duct and lingual nerve lie between the deep part of the gland and hyoglossus

Where would you place a skin incision to remove the submandibular gland?

I would place my incision well below the lower border of the mandible.

Why would you place your skin incision there?

To avoid damage to the marginal mandibular branch of the facial nerve which runs along the lower border of the mandible.

What is the effect of damaging this nerve?

The marginal mandibular branch supplies the muscles of the lower lip so that damage would result in drooping of the mouth.

9. THE ROOT OF THE NECK

What symptoms does a cervical rib cause?

A cervical rib may not cause any problems and thus be asymptomatic. However, if symptomatic a cervical rib may cause thoracic outlet obstruction. The clinical features are determined by the structure that is compressed.

- Compression of the subclavian artery may cause trophic changes, rest pain and even gangrene (Raynaud's phenomenon)
- Venous compression causes arm swelling
- Compression of the C8 and T1 nerve roots cause pain and paraesthesia in the ulnar aspect of the forearm and upper arm, with weakness and wasting of the small muscles of the hand

What are the operative complications of removing a cervical rib?

The complications are local and systemic. The important complications are the local ones which may involve damage to the numerous vital structures at the root of the neck.

- **Immediate complications** include haemorrhage and pneumothorax
- **Early complications** are haematoma formation with resultant compression of the subclavian artery and vein, the T1 nerve root and sympathetic chain causing a Horner's syndrome

What are the relations of the stellate ganglion?

Posteriorly lies the head of the 1st rib and the base of the transverse process of C7. Anteriorly lies the apex of the pleura.

What are the important relations of scalenus anterior?

The phrenic nerve passes vertically down the front of the scalenus anterior. It is plastered to the muscle by the overlying pre-vertebral fascia.

Anterior to the pre-vertebral fascia lie

- The transcervical and suprascapular arteries
- The vagus nerve in the carotid sheath
- The recurrent laryngeal nerve on the right side

Behind scalenus anterior lies the 2nd part subclavian artery and the anterior rami of the lower cervical and 1st thoracic nerves.

10.   DIAPHRAGM

Can you briefly describe the embryological development of the diaphragm?

The diaphragm is formed by fusion of the septum transversum (which forms the central tendon) and the dorsal oesophageal mesentery (which forms the connective tissue around the oesophageal and vena caval openings). The connective tissue of the periphery of the diaphragm is formed from the pleuro-peritoneal membranes and mesoderm of the dorsal body wall. The central tendon is derived from this connective tissue. The rest of the diaphragm is invaded through the transverse septum by muscle cells from the 3rd, 4th and 5th cervical myotomes.

What are the main openings in the diaphragm?

The diaphragm has three main openings.

The **aortic opening** is situated opposite the T12 vertebra and transmits the aorta, the azygos vein and the thoracic duct.

The **oesophageal opening** is at the level of the T10 vertebra and is situated between the muscular fibres of the right crus of the diaphragm and transmits the left gastric artery and vein and two vagal trunks.

The **vena caval opening** is at the level of the T8 vertebra and is just to the right of the midline lying in the central tendon. The right phrenic nerve pierces the central tendon alongside the inferior vena cava at this opening.

Does the diaphragm have any other openings?

The diaphragm has several smaller openings for the

*   Splanchnic nerves (which pierce each crus)
*   Sympathetic trunk (behind the medial arcuate ligament)
*   Subcostal nerve and vessels (behind the lateral arcuate ligament)
*   Left phrenic nerve
*   Superior epigastric vessels (behind the xiphisternum and cross the fibres of the diaphragm)
*   Extraperitoneal lymph vessels

What is the nerve supply to the diaphragm?

Each half of the diaphragm is supplied by its own **phrenic nerve** (C3–C5 but predominantly C4). The **lower intercostal nerve** sends some proprioceptive fibres to the periphery of the diaphragm. The motor supply is derived solely from the phrenic nerves.

What is the function of the diaphragm?

The major function of the diaphragm is to aid inspiration, but it is also involved in abdominal straining, i.e. the act of defaecation, micturition, parturition. (The diaphragm is not involved in expiration.)

Where are the common sites of hernia formation in the diaphragm?

Congenital hernia may form in sites of potential defects. These include

- The **foramen of Bochdalek** (posteriorly where the lumbar and costal elements fail to fuse)
- The **foramen of Morgagni** (anterior defect between the xiphoid and costal margins)
- A deficiency in the whole central tendon, or a congenitally large oesophageal hiatus

Acquired hiatus herniae are far more common than congenital abnormalities and consist of the sliding or rolling types.

11. PAROTID GLAND

Can you describe the important anatomical relations of the parotid gland?

The parotid gland is the largest salivary gland and fills the gap between the mastoid process, the mandible and the styloid process, extending variably onto the masseter, sternocleido-mastoid, posterior belly of digastric and medial pterygoid.

Above the parotid gland lies the external auditory meatus and temporo-mandibular joint. Below, the parotid overlaps the posterior belly of digastric. Medially lies the styloid process. Posteriorly, the parotid overflows the sternocleidomastoid and anteriorly it overlies the mandible with the overlying masseter.

What structures lie within the parotid gland?

The **facial nerve**, **retromandibular vein** and **external carotid artery** all lie within the parotid gland. The facial nerve is the most superficial structure and the carotid artery the deepest of these structures. Within the facial gland there are lymph nodes and branches of the auriculotemporal nerve.

What is the relation of the facial nerve to the parotid gland?

The facial nerve emerges from the stylomastoid foramen and winds laterally to the styloid process. Just beyond the bony part of the external auditory meatus and the mastoid process, the facial nerve dives into the posterior aspect of the parotid gland and bifurcates almost immediately into its two main divisions. The upper division (divides into **temporal** and **zygomatic** branches), the lower division gives rise to the **buccal**, **mandibular** and **cervical** branches. (An important point to note is that the branches of the facial nerve emerge from behind the anterior border of the parotid gland, not from the lateral surface.) The branches of the facial nerve emerge on the anterior aspect of the parotid to lie on the masseter and so pass to the muscles of the face. No branches emerge from the superficial aspect of the gland.

Where does the parotid duct open in the mouth?

The parotid duct opens opposite the upper second molar tooth having run forward across the masseter and pierced buccinator.

What is the secretomotor supply of the parotid gland?

Pre-ganglionic secretor motor fibres arise from cell bodies in the **inferior salivatory nucleus** of the medulla and pass via the glossopharyngeal nerve, its tympanic branch, the tympanic plexus and the lesser petrosal nerve to the **otic ganglion**. Secretomotor fibres arising from the cell bodies in the otic ganglion reach the parotid gland along the auriculotemporal nerve.

12.   PANCREAS AND SPLEEN

What is the investigation pictured below?

This is a contrast CT scan of the abdomen.

Can you name the labelled structures?

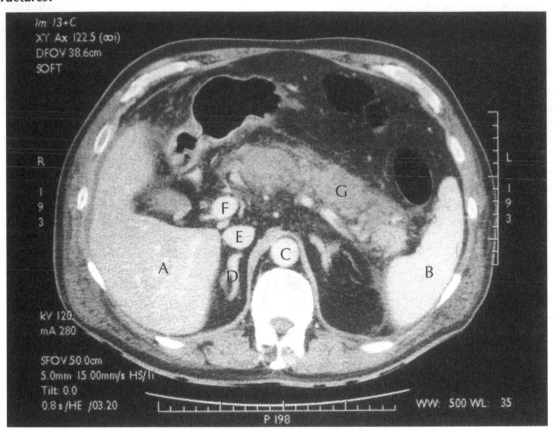

A. Liver	E. Inferior Vena Cava
B. Spleen	F. Portal vein
C. Aorta	G. Pancreas
D. Adrenal gland	

What are the important posterior relations of the pancreas?

The pancreas is a retroperitoneal organ lying roughly in the trans-pyloric plane. It can be divided into a head, neck, body and tail. The **head of the pancreas** (at the level of L2 vertebra) lies over the **inferior vena cava**, the **right and left renal veins**, the terminal part of the **common bile duct** and the **superior mesenteric vein and artery**.

The **neck of the pancreas** lies (at the level of L1 vertebra) in front of the **superior mesenteric and portal veins**.

The **body of the pancreas** overlies the **left renal vein**, **aorta**, **left crus of the diaphragm**, **left psoas muscle**, pole of the **left adrenal gland** and the hilum of the **left kidney**. The tortuous splenic artery runs along its upper border. The **tail of the pancreas** lies in front of the **hilum of the left kidney**.

What is the arterial blood supply to the pancreas?

The main arterial blood supply to the pancreas comes from the **splenic artery** which gives off branches to the neck, body and tail. The head of the pancreas is supplied by the superior and inferior **pancreaticoduodenal arteries**.

What viscera may be injured when performing a splenectomy?

During a splenectomy one must beware of injuring the stomach, colon, left kidney and the tail of the pancreas.

What important ligaments can be found around the spleen?

The two important ligaments that are found around the spleen are the **lienorenal** and **gastrosplenic ligaments**.

What runs in these ligaments?

The **lienorenal** ligament attaches the spleen to the posterior abdominal wall and carries the splenic vessels and tail of the pancreas. The **gastrosplenic** ligament attaches the spleen to the greater curvature of the stomach and carries the short gastric and left gastroepiploic vessels.

Where do accessory spleens occur?

Accessory spleens are most commonly found near the hilum of the spleen, but may also be found in the tail of the pancreas, omentum, small bowel mesentery, ovary and testis.

How common are accessory spleens?

They occur in approximately 10% of patients.

13.   VASCULAR SUPPLY OF THE LARGE BOWEL

What is the arterial blood supply of the colon?

The arterial blood supply of the large bowel arises from two main vessels: the **superior mesenteric** (supplies midgut structures) and **inferior mesenteric arteries** (supplies hindgut structures). The superior mesenteric artery gives off three major branches: the **middle colic**, **right colic** and **ileocolic** arteries. These three branches supply the right side of the colon to the mid-transverse colon. The inferior mesenteric artery gives off the **left colic** artery and **sigmoidal** branches, which supply the remainder of the colon.

At what level are the proximal origins of the superior and inferior mesenteric arteries?

The superior mesenteric artery arises from the aorta at the level of **L1**. The inferior mesenteric artery arises from the aorta at the level of **L3**.

Is there any vascular connection between these two mesenteric arteries?

Yes, there is an important anastomosis between these two arterial systems, consisting of a continuous vascular arcade which runs along the whole length of the large bowel and is called the **marginal artery of Drummond**.

What is the venous drainage of the large bowel?

The venous drainage is through the **inferior mesenteric** and **superior mesenteric veins**. The inferior mesenteric vein ascends above the point of origin of its artery and enters the splenic vein behind the pancreas. The superior mesenteric vein joins the splenic vein behind the neck of the pancreas in the transpyloric plane, to form the portal vein. The **portal vein** ascends behind the first part of the duodenum, through the free edge of the lesser sac into the porta hepatis.

Where do porto-systemic anastomoses occur?

The potential sites for porto-systemic anastomoses include

- The oesophageal branch of the left gastric vein and the oesophageal veins of the azygos system
- The portal tributaries, the mesentery and the mesocolon
- The retroperitoneal and phrenic veins
- The superior haemorrhoidal branch of the inferior mesenteric vein and the inferior haemorrhoidal veins draining into the internal iliac vein
- Portal branches in the liver and the veins of the diaphragm across the bare area of the liver
- Portal branches of the liver and veins of the abdominal wall or veins passing along the falciform ligament to the umbilicus (these may result in formation of dilated veins called caput Medusae)

14. FEMORAL TRIANGLE

What are the boundaries of the femoral triangle?

The femoral triangle is bound **superiorly** by the inguinal ligament, **medially** by the medial border of adductor longus and **laterally** by the medial border of sartorius. The **floor of the triangle** consists of iliacus, tendon of pectineus, psoas and adductor longus. The **roof** is formed by superficial fascia, containing superficial lymph nodes, the saphenous vein with its tributaries and the fascia lata.

What are the contents of the femoral triangle?

The contents of the femoral triangle are the

- Femoral artery
- Femoral vein
- Femoral nerve
- Deep inguinal lymph nodes

What is the relationship between the femoral sheath and a femoral hernia?

The medial part of the femoral sheath contains a small vertical gap called the femoral canal, through which a femoral hernia may arise. Lateral to the femoral canal, but still within the femoral sheath, lies the femoral vein and lateral to that, the femoral artery.

What do you normally find in the femoral canal?

The femoral canal usually contains extra-peritoneal fat and a constant lymph node called Cloquet's node.

What are the boundaries of the femoral canal?

The boundaries of the femoral canal are

- **Medially**: the sharp edge of the pectineal part of the inguinal ligament
- **Laterally**: the femoral vein
- **Posteriorly**: the pectineal ligament of Astley Cooper
- **Anteriorly**: the inguinal ligament

15.   VERTEBRAE AND THE VERTEBRAL COLUMN

What are the general characteristics of the vertebra?

- All vertebrae consist of a body and a dorsal neural arch, between which is the vertebral foramen. (NB. The vertebral canal is formed only when all of the vertebrae are strung together as a column.)
- **Three processes** arise from the neural arch: the spinous process and two transverse processes
- The **lamina** is the part of the neural arch between the spinous and transverse processes
- The **pedicle** is the part of the neural arch between the transverse process and the body
- The **facet joints** are synovial joints between the neural arches of adjacent vertebrae. They are at the root of the transverse process (i.e. the junction between the lamina and pedicle).

How can you distinguish between typical cervical, thoracic and lumbar vertebrae?

The presence or absence of two particular anatomical features allows one to distinguish between these three types of vertebrae. The two features are a foramen in the transverse process and the presence of a costal facet joint. Only typical cervical vertebrae will have a foramen in the transverse process, only typical thoracic vertebrae will have a costal facet (for articulation with a rib) and only typical lumbar vertebrae will have neither of these features.

What joints are formed in the vertebral column?

The vertebral column has two types of articulation, firstly **between vertebral bodies**, and secondly **between neural arches**.

- The joints between the adjacent vertebral bodies are secondary cartilaginous joints or symphyses.
- The joints between the arches are between the articular facets of the superior articular process of one vertebra and the inferior facets of the inferior articular process of the vertebra above. They are termed zygopophyseal joints or more commonly facet joints. The articular facets are found at the root of the transverse process. (NB. They should not be confused with the costal facets of thoracic vertebrae which form the articulation with the ribs.)

What is the most common site for a prolapsed disc?

The most common site for a prolapsed disc is L5/S1. The commonest direction of prolapse is postero-lateral.

How is disc prolapse and level of nerve root compression related?

The L5 nerve root hugs the pedicle of L5 and emerges from the intervertebral foramen (between the pedicles of L5 and S1). Therefore, the L5 nerve root has exited before it reaches the postero-lateral prolapse. Thus, it is the S1 nerve root that is affected by L5/S1 prolapse. This rule also applies more proximally in the spine so that a L4/L5 disc prolapse usually affects the L5 nerve root and a C6/7 disc affects the C7 nerve root.

16.   ARTERIAL SUPPLY OF THE LOWER LIMB

What is the arterial blood supply of the lower limb?

The main arterial supply to the lower limb is from the **femoral artery**, a continuation of the external iliac artery beyond the inguinal ligament. The femoral artery begins at the mid-inguinal point (midway between the symphysis pubis and the anterior iliac spine) and divides into two main branches, just below the femoral sheath (3.5 cm below the inguinal ligament), into the superficial femoral and profunda femoris arteries.

- The **superficial femoral** artery has no major branches in the thigh and passes into the adductor canal to form the popliteal artery at the adductor hiatus
- The **profunda femoris** artery runs deep in the thigh. It is the main arterial supply of the thigh. It branches into medial and lateral circumflex femoral arteries to supply the proximal thigh and has four perforating branches along its length until its termination.

What is the investigation shown below?

Trans-femoral digital subtraction angiogram of the lower limb.

Can you name the labelled structures?

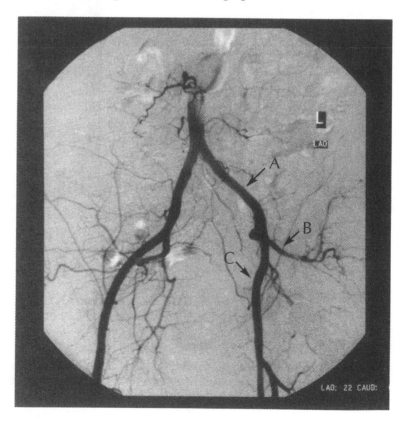

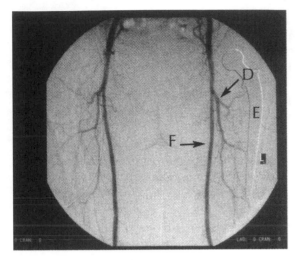

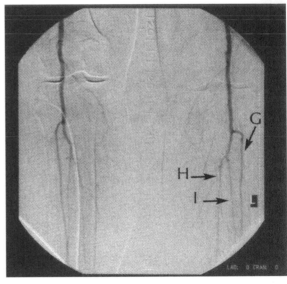

A. Common iliac artery	F. Superficial femoral artery
B. Internal iliac artery	G. Anterior tibial artery
C. External iliac artery	H. Posterior tibial artery
D. Profunda femoris	I. Peroneal artery
E. Femoral prosthesis of a total hip replacement	

Can you describe the course and relations of the popliteal artery?

The popliteal artery is a continuation of the femoral artery after it has passed through the adductor hiatus.

- The popliteal artery enters the popliteal fossa and lies on the medial aspect of the femur, almost in contact with the bone. Distally, it lies on the posterior capsule of the knee joint and popliteus. The popliteal vein and tibial nerve are more superficial.

- The popliteal artery branches into three genicular branches on the medial side (superior medial, middle and inferior medial) and two genicular branches on the lateral side (superior and inferior). It ends as it passes under the fibrous arch of soleus, immediately dividing into anterior and posterior tibial arteries.

What structures form the borders of the popliteal fossa?

The popliteal fossa is diamond shaped and lies behind the knee. The borders are

- **Supero-laterally**: tendon of biceps femoris
- **Supero-medially**: tendons of semimembranosus and semitendinosus
- **Infero-laterally**: lateral head of gastrocnemius
- **Infero-medially**: medial head of gastrocnemius

What does the popliteal fossa contain?

The popliteal fossa contains the tibial and common peroneal nerves, the popliteal artery and vein. A group of lymph nodes is also found within the fossa. The popliteal artery is the deepest structure within the fossa.

At all levels, the popliteal vein lies between the artery and the tibial nerve. The tibial nerve runs vertically along the middle of the fossa. The common peroneal nerve runs along the upper lateral border of the fossa, adjacent to biceps femoris, exiting the fossa at the lateral apex, running over the lateral head of gastrocnemius and disappearing into the substance of peroneus longus.

What is the arterial supply of the foot?

The arterial blood supply to the foot comes from the **anterior** and **posterior tibial arteries**.

- The anterior tibial artery crosses the ankle anteriorly, beneath the extensor retinaculum, midway between the malleoli to become the dorsalis pedis artery. Initially, it lies between the tibialis anterior (medially) and extensor digitorum longus (laterally), then between tibialis anterior and extensor hallucis longus. It forms the dorsal arch artery.
- The **posterior tibial artery** provides the **main blood supply to the foot**. At the ankle it runs posterior to the medial malleolus between the tendon of flexor hallucis longus and the posterior tibial nerve. It passes deep to the flexor retinaculum to divide into the medial and lateral plantar arteries.

17.   THE BREAST

What are the anatomical borders of the female breast?

The breast extends from the second to the sixth rib in the mid-clavicular line. It lies over the pectoralis major and extends to lie on the serratus anterior and external oblique muscles.

Can you describe the duct arrangement in the breast?

In the normal breast, there are approximately **15 ducts** which open separately onto the summit of the nipple. Each duct has a dilated ampulla beneath the areola and each duct drains a lobe of the breast. The lobes of the breast are separated by fibres which radiate out from the centre.

What is the arterial blood supply of the breast?

The blood supply of the breast is derived from the **lateral thoracic artery**, **internal thoracic artery** and the **thoracoacromial artery**. Branches of the lateral thoracic artery curl round the border of the pectoralis major. The internal thoracic artery sends branches through the intercostal spaces (2nd and 3rd spaces are largest). There may be some small perforated branches from the intercostal arteries. The thoracoacromial artery mainly supplies the upper part of the breast.

Can you describe the lymphatic drainage of the breast?

Most of the lymph of the breast drains through the axilla. Lymph from the lateral part of the breast (upper and lower outer quadrants) drains to the axilla and infra-clavicular nodes and that from the medial part (upper and lower inner quadrants) drain through the intercostal spaces into the internal thoracic (parasternal) nodes. However, there can be significant lymph flow between the lateral and medial parts of the breast and vice versa. In addition, there is a rich anastomosing network of lymphatic capillaries continuous with capillaries of the opposite breast and with the abdominal wall. Hence, lymph may drain to the opposite axilla to the peritoneal cavity and liver through the diaphragm or even to the inguinal lymph nodes.

18.   CORONARY ARTERIES

What is the origin of the coronary arteries?

The **left coronary artery** arises from the **left posterior aortic sinus** behind the pulmonary trunk. It emerges between the left auricular appendage and the infundibulum of the right ventricle. The **right coronary artery** arises from the **anterior aortic sinus** and passes between the right auricle and infundibulum of the right ventricle.

What are the branches of the right coronary artery?

The right coronary artery gives off branches in both the right atrium and ventricle. It gives off the **conus artery** and **SA-nodal artery** at the inferior border of the heart. The right coronary artery also gives off the **right marginal artery** which passes to the left along the right ventricle. On the diaphragmatic surface of the heart, the right coronary artery continues as the **posterior interventricular artery** (posterior descending artery).

What are the main branches of the left coronary artery?

Following a short course, the left coronary artery divides into two main branches, the **circumflex branch** and the **left anterior descending** (anterior interventricular artery). The left anterior descending artery runs down in the interventricular groove to the apex of the heart. It gives off several large ventricular branches called **diagonals**. The circumflex artery continues to the back of the heart in the atrioventricular groove giving off various ventricular branches called **obtuse marginals**.

Are there any anastomoses between the two main coronary arteries?

Yes, anastomoses do occur between the left and right coronary arteries, through terminal arterioles in the atrioventricular groove and between the interventricular branches. However, the anastomoses on the surface of the heart are insignificant. Potential anastomoses may be found between the coronary arteries and pericardial arteries around the roots of the great vessels.

Can you briefly describe the venous drainage of the heart?

The venous drainage of the heart may be divided into three main groups

*   The **coronary sinus**
*   The **anterior cardiac veins**
*   The **venae cordis minimae**

The **coronary sinus** receives five tributaries: the great, middle and small cardiac veins, the posterior vein of the left ventricle and the oblique vein of the left atrium. The coronary sinus lies on the posterior part of the interventricular groove and receives 60% of the blood supply of the heart. The coronary sinus opens at its lower end into the posterior wall of the right atrium to the left of the inferior vena caval opening. The **anterior cardiac veins** are a series of veins that run across the surface of the right ventricle and open into the right atrium. The **venae cordis minimae** are numerous small veins in the walls of all the chambers of the heart that open directly into the cardiac chambers.

19.   AXILLARY NODE SAMPLING

What do you understand by the term axillary node clearance?

Axillary node clearance is an established procedure for control of metastatic disease in invasive breast cancer. It can provide prognostic information and influence adjuvant therapy. Axillary node clearance can be defined as clearing the axillary contents bounded by the axillary skin laterally, latissimus dorsi, teres major and subscapularis muscles posteriorly, the lower border of the axillary vein superiorly, pectoralis major and minor anteriorly and the chest wall medially.

How might you anatomically classify the position of axillary nodes?

The level of axillary nodes may be anatomically defined to three levels – level I, II and III. **Level I nodes** are those that are inferior and lateral to pectoralis minor, **level II nodes** posterior to pectoralis minor and **level III** supero-medial to pectoralis minor. It is important to note that all these nodes are in continuity with one another.

Can you describe how you would carry out a level II axillary clearance?

With informed consent from the patient, the side of the operation is marked with an indelible marker pen and the patient given prophylaxis against deep vein thrombosis. The patient is positioned supine with the arm abducted and placed on an arm board 90° to the chest wall.

A lazy 'S' skin excision is made in the axilla. Skin flaps are raised (1 cm) with the anterior margin skin flap adjacent to the lateral wall of the pectoralis minor and the posterior margin skin flap adjacent to latissimus dorsi. This dissection is continued to the lower border of the axillary vein, which is exposed. The axillary contents are dissected free from the lateral border and behind pectoralis minor. Care is taken to preserve the lateral pectoral neurovascular bundle. The axillary contents are then separated from the medial wall of the axilla. During dissection, the intercostal brachial nerve may be seen and should be preserved if possible. A pyramidal block of tissue containing the lymph nodes may now be removed.

What nerves may be encountered during an axillary dissection?

The nerve to serratus anterior (long thoracic nerve) of Bell, the nerve to latissimus dorsi (thoraco-dorsal nerve) and the intercostal brachial nerve.

20.   LUMBAR VERTEBRAE

How many lumbar vertebrae are there in the normal spinal column?

Five.

Can you describe the characteristics of a lumbar vertebra?

Lumbar vertebra are characterised by the

- large size of their bodies
- absence of costal facets on the bodies and the transverse processes
- triangular vertebral foramen
- quadrangular or hatchet shaped spinous process that points backwards
- superior articular process that is vertical, curved, faces backwards and medially, and possesses a mamillary process at the posterior rim

How can you differentiate the L5 vertebra from the other lumbar vertabrae?

The L5 vertebra is unique in that the transverse process unites directly with the side of the body as well as the pedicle.

What is attached to the lumbar transverse processes?

The **psoas fascia** and the anterior layer of the **lumbar fascia** are attached to the four lumbar transverse processes. The medial and **lateral arcuate** ligaments are also attached to the ridge on the L1 transverse process. The transverse process of the fifth lumbar vertebrae has the strong **iliolumbar ligament** attached, through which the quadratus lumborum muscle arises.

What is meant by the term sacralisation?

Sacralisation is a condition where the fifth lumbar vertebrae is fused on one or both sides to the first sacral vertebra.

21.   TRANS-PYLORIC PLANE OF ADDISON

What is the trans-pyloric plane of Addison?

The trans-pyloric plane of Addison is a point mid-way between the supra-sternal notch of the manubrium and the upper border of the symphysis pubis. In clinical practice it corresponds to a **hand's breadth below the xiphoid process**.

Which vertebra lies at this level?

This plane passes through the body of the first lumbar vertebra.

What important structures are seen at this level?

*   Hilum of the kidneys and their vascular pedicles
*   Termination of the spinal cord
*   Junction of the superior mesenteric and splenic veins to form the origin of the portal vein
*   Origin of the superior mesenteric artery at the aorta and the neck of the pancreas
*   Front of the gall bladder at the costal margin

At what vertebral level do you find the origin of the inferior mesenteric artery?

The origin of the inferior mesenteric artery is at the level of the **third lumbar vertebra**. This is also known as at the soft costal plane, which passes across lower margins of thoracic cage formed by the 10th costal cartilage on each side.

At what level does the aorta bifurcate?

The aorta bifurcates at the level of the fourth and fifth lumbar vertebrae, slightly to the left of the mid-line.

What is the relationship between the common iliac artery, vein and ureter?

The common iliac arteries are slightly anterior to the common iliac veins. The distal ureter passes anterior to both these vessels.

22.   SHOULDER JOINT AND ARM

Can you describe the humerus?

In the anatomical position, the humeral head faces medially and backwards.

Between the greater and lesser tuberosities lies the intertubercular groove, through which the tendon of the long head of biceps runs. Distally, the articular surfaces are the trochlea (articulates with the trochlear notch of the ulna) and the capitulum (articulates with the upper surface of the head of the radius). Superior to the trochlea is the coronoid fossa which accepts the tip of the coronoid process during full flexion.

What do you find in the anterior compartment of the arm?

- **Muscles**: these include the flexors (biceps, brachialis) and adductor (coracobrachialis) muscles
- **Nerves and vessels**: the main neurovascular bundle from the axilla enters the anterior compartment with the exception of the radial nerve and profunda brachii artery which both enter the posterior (extensor) compartment. However, the radial nerve does enter the lower part of the anterior compartment from the posterior compartment.

What are the attachments of the biceps muscle?

Biceps has **two proximal origins**: the **supra-glenoid tubercle** for the long head (tendon runs in the intertubercular groove) and the **coracoid process of the scapula** for the short head.
The **insertion** is the **bicipital tuberosity of the radius**.

What do you find in the posterior compartment of the arm?

- **Muscles**: the only muscle within this compartment is the triceps
- **Nerve and vessels**: radial nerve and profunda brachii artery. The ulnar nerve runs through the lower part of this compartment.

What is the course of the ulnar nerve in the arm?

The ulnar nerve runs through the lower part of the extensor (posterior) compartment and disappears into the forearm between the two heads of flexor carpi ulnaris.

What are the common causes of an axillary nerve injury?

The common causes of an axillary nerve injury include

- **Anterior dislocation of the shoulder**
- **Proximal humeral fracture**
- **Misplaced hypodermic needle injections** into the deltoid muscle

What are the effects of an axillary nerve injury?

The effects of axillary nerve injury are

- Paralysis of the deltoid muscle
- Almost complete loss of shoulder abduction
- Loss of sensation over the 'badge area'.

23.   RADIAL NERVE

What is the origin of the radial nerve?

The radial nerve is the **continuation of the posterior cord** of the brachial plexus. The posterior cord contains fibres from all the nerve roots of the brachial plexus (C5–T1).

What is its course in the arm?

The radial nerve runs with the profunda brachii artery along the spiral groove of the humerus in the **posterior compartment of the arm**. It pierces the lateral inter-muscular septum at the mid point of the humerus to enter the anterior compartment of the arm. After entering the lateral side of the cubital fossa it divides into its terminal branches over the lateral epicondyle.

What are the terminal branches of the radial nerve?

There are two terminal branches of the radial nerve: the **superficial radial nerve** (predominantly sensory) and the deep branch or **posterior interosseous nerve** (predominantly motor).

Can you describe the course of the superficial radial nerve in the forearm and the hand?

From the cubital fossa, the superficial radial nerve runs with the radial artery underneath brachioradialis. Its terminal branches pass superficial to the tendons of the anatomical snuff box (abductor pollicis longus, extensor pollicis brevis and extensor pollicis longus) to supply the dorsum of the hand and the extensor surface of the lateral 3½ digits.

What is the course of the deep branch (posterior interosseous) in the forearm?

From the cubital fossa, the posterior interosseous nerve passes between the two heads of supinator, approximately 3 cm distal to the head of the radius and runs into the posterior compartment of the forearm. It has a deep course on the interosseous membrane all the way to the wrist joint. It divides to supply the deep and superficial muscles of the posterior (extensor) compartment.

NB. Extensor carpi radialis longus and brachioradialis are supplied by the main radial nerve from just above the elbow.

How might you test radial nerve function?

Cutaneous sensibility may be tested over the skin of the anatomical snuff box including that over the first dorsal interosseous (the only area that is reliably supplied by the superficial radial nerve).
Motor function may be tested by dorsi-flexion of the wrist.

24.   MEDIAN NERVE

What does the median nerve supply in the hand?

The **motor component** of the median nerve supplies 1st and 2nd lumbricals, opponens pollicis, abductor pollicis brevis and flexor pollicis brevis (LOAF). The **sensory component** of the median nerve supplies the palmar skin of the radial 3½ digits.

What are the contents of the carpal tunnel?

The carpal tunnel contains the median nerve and 10 tendons.

- Flexor digitorum superficialis (x 4)
- Flexor digitorum profundus (x 4)
- Flexor pollicis longus (x 1)
- Flexor carpi radialis (x 1)

Why is the recurrent motor branch of the median nerve important?

The recurrent motor branch is important because it exits the carpal tunnel and supplies the thenar muscles: abductor pollicis brevis, flexor pollicis brevis and opponens pollicis. Therefore, carpal tunnel syndrome may lead to thenar muscle wasting. In addition, the recurrent motor branch, as a result of its course, may be damaged during decompression surgery (i.e. beware of extending the incision too far to the radial side of the carpal tunnel).

What is the importance of the palmar cutaneous branch of the median nerve?

The superficial palmar branch crosses the wrist joint superficial to the flexor retinaculum to supply the palmar skin over the thenar eminence. It should therefore be unaffected in patients with carpal tunnel syndrome.

What does the median nerve supply in the forearm?

The median nerve in the forearm supplies the majority of the long flexors (flexor carpi radialis, palmaris longus, flexor digitorum superficialis) and via its anterior interosseus branch.

- The flexor pollicis longus
- Radial half of flexor digitorum profundus
- Pronator quadratus

It also supplies the interosseous membrane and periosteum of the radius and ulna. (The median nerve does not have a cutaneous branch in the forearm.)

What is the cutaneous supply of the forearm?

- Medial cutaneous nerve of the forearm (a direct branch of the medial cord)
- Lateral cutaneous nerve of the forearm (branch of the musculocutaneous nerve)
- Posterior cutaneous nerve of the forearm (branch of the radial nerve)

What is the course of the median nerve in the forearm?

The median nerve passes beneath the bicipital aponeurosis at the elbow. It divides into two branches after leaving the ante-cubital fossa (the brachial artery and veins, biceps tendon and radial nerve all lie lateral to it) between the two heads of pronator teres (which forms the medial border of the cubital fossa). The anterior interosseous branch runs with the anterior interosseous artery. The remaining nerve runs on the deep surface of flexor digitorum superficialis and ends in the anterior part of the capsule of the wrist and carpal joints.

25.   FOREARM ANATOMY

What muscles are attached to the common flexor origin?

The **superficial muscles** arise from the common flexor origin. From medial to lateral

- Pronator teres
- Flexor carpi radialis
- Palmaris longus
- Flexor digitorum superficialis
- Flexor carpi ulnaris

What other muscles are found in the anterior compartment of the forearm?

The **deep muscles** arise from the **interosseous membrane** and the volar surface of the radius and ulna

- Flexor pollicis longus
- Flexor digitorum profundus
- Pronator quadratus

What are the boundaries of the ante-cubital fossa?

The ante-cubital fossa is an inter-muscular space between **brachioradialis** (laterally), **pronator teres** (medially) and an imaginary line between the **two epicondyles**. The floor is formed by the brachialis muscle.

What are the contents of the antecubital fossa?

From **medial to lateral**

- Median nerve (the median nerve is the most medial structure)
- Brachial artery and accompanying veins
- Terminal branches of the radial nerve (may be seen beneath the edge of the brachioradialis)

What innervates the flexor muscles in the forearm?

The majority of the forearm flexors are innervated by the **median nerve** (flexor carpi radialis, palmaris longus, flexor digitorum superficialis, flexor pollicis longus, radial half of flexor digitorum profundus). The remainder are innervated by the **ulnar nerve** (medial half of flexor digitorum profundus and flexor carpi ulnaris).

What is the effect of an ulnar nerve injury behind the elbow?

Injuries to the ulnar nerve at the elbow are usually due to local trauma and fracture dislocations. The effect is

- A motor loss affecting the ulnar half of flexor digitorum profundus and flexor carpi ulnaris in the forearm, the three hypothenar muscles, the two lumbricals on the ulnar side, all the interossei and both heads of adductor pollicis in the hand.

This results in a clawed hand due to

- Loss of flexion at the MCP joints due to paralysis of the small muscles of the hand
- Flexion of the IP joints (due to paralysis of the interossei and lumbricals which normally flex the MCP joints and extend the IP joints) is still present because FDS is spared

The sensory loss affects the digital nerve supply to the little and ulnar half of the ring finger.

Can you describe the cutaneous supply of the forearm?

The cutaneous supply can be considered in terms of the dermatomes.

- The central dermatome of the upper limb is C7. In the forearm, this supplies a thin strip of skin in the middle of the extensor surface from the elbow to the wrist. The C6 and C8 dermatomes supply the remainder of the skin. Their territories join in the middle of the flexor surface, at the axial line of the upper limb with C6 supplying the radial side and C8 supplying the ulnar side.
- The peripheral sensory nerves are the posterior cutaneous nerve of the forearm (a branch of the radial nerve) supplying a thin strip on the extensor surface, the medial and lateral cutaneous nerves of the forearm (from the medial cord and the musculocutaneous nerve respectively).

26.   WRIST JOINT

What is the normal volar tilt of the radius?	The normal volar tilt of the distal radius is approximately 12°.
Why is this important?	This is particularly important when assessing dorsal angulation of wrist fractures. Generally, manipulation of a Colles' fracture is recommended if the distal fragment is angulated dorsally >12° from the shaft of the radius.
What is the tubercle of Lister?	The tubercle of Lister is a prominent bony ridge located on the dorsal surface of the distal radius. On the ulnar side of the tubercle lies a groove for the tendon of extensor pollicis longus. On the radial side of the tubercle lie grooves for the tendons of extensor carpi radialis brevis and longus.
Which carpal bones articulate with the distal radius?	The scaphoid, lunate and triquetral.
	Articulation between these carpal bones and the distal radius forms the wrist joint. Although the triquetral only articulates with the distal radius in extreme adduction of the wrist, it is always recognised as part of the wrist joint. (The wrist joint is a separate anatomical entity from the distal radio-ulnar joint.)
What is the flexor retinaculum?	The flexor retinaculum is a strong band attached to four bony points on the flexor aspect of the wrist.
What are these bony points?	These bony points are

- The scaphoid tubercle and the trapezium on the radial side
- The pisiform and hook of the hamate on the ulnar side

Can you briefly describe the important anatomical relations of the flexor retinaculum?	The muscles of the thenar and hypothenar eminence arise from the flexor retinaculum and a number of structures pass across it, both superficially and deep.

Superficial to the flexor retinaculum are **two nerves**, **two arteries** and **one tendon**

- **On the ulnar side**, the ulnar nerve and artery pass superficially, but are bridged by a slender band of tissue from the flexor retinaculum, to form the canal of Guyon
- **On the radial side**, the palmar branch of the median nerve and the superficial palmar branch of the radial artery cross the retinaculum. The palmaris longus tendon is fused to the midline of the retinaculum as it passes distally to expand into the palmar aponeurosis.

Deep to the flexor retinaculum lies the carpal tunnel within which are the **median nerve and 10 tendons**. These tendons are

- Flexor digitorum superficialis (x 4)
- Flexor digitorum profundus (x 4)
- Flexor pollicis longus (x 1)
- Flexor carpi radialis (x 1)

What are the borders and important relations of the anatomical snuff box?

The anatomical snuff box lies between the extensor pollicis longus tendon on the ulnar side and the tendons of extensor pollicis brevis and abductor pollicis longus on the radial side.

- The cutaneous branches of the radial nerve cross these tendons to supply sensation over the first dorsal interosseus muscle
- The radial artery lies in the floor of the snuff box, deep to all three tendons
- The palpable bony points are radial styloid proximally and the base of the thumb metacarpal distally, between these two structures, the scaphoid and trapezium can be palpated.

27.   SCIATIC NERVE AND THE HIP JOINT

What nerve roots form the sciatic nerve?

The sciatic nerve is formed from the nerve roots of the lumbosacral trunk (L4 and L5) and the upper sacral plexus (S1, S2, S3).

What are the main branches of the sciatic nerve?

The main branches of the sciatic nerve are a **branch to the posterior compartment of the thigh**, **the common peroneal nerve and the tibial nerve**.

What do they supply?

The **branch to the posterior compartment of the thigh** supplies the muscles within this compartment, namely

- The **short external rotators of the hip joint** (gemelli, obturator internus, quadratus femoris)
- **Hamstrings** (semitendinosus, semimembranosus, biceps femoris, hamstring half of adductor magnus)

The **common peroneal nerve** supplies the muscles of the anterior (via deep peroneal nerve) and peroneal (via superficial peroneal nerve) compartments and sensation to the antero-lateral leg and dorsum of the foot. (NB. The term leg applies to the lower limb below the knee.)

The **tibial nerve** supplies the muscles of the posterior compartments (superficial and deep) of the leg and sensation to the posterior region of the leg and sole of the foot.

Can you describe the posterior surgical approach to the hip joint?

- The skin incision is centred on the posterior part of the greater trochanter. Proximally, it is curved towards the posterior superior iliac spine and distally it follows the femoral shaft.
- After the subcutaneous fat, the fascia lata is encountered. Proximally, the fascia lata blends into the gluteus maximus. After the fascia lata is split, the muscles covering the posterior aspect of the hip joint are seen.
- The sciatic nerve is identified between gluteus maximus and the short external rotators of the hip (superior and inferior gemelli, piriformis and obturator internus). These tendons are divided to display the posterior capsule of the hip joint.

Where does the hip joint capsule attach to the femur?

The capsule of the hip joint is attached anteriorly to the inter-trochanteric line, and posteriorly it is attached halfway along the femoral neck.

What are the ligaments of the hip joint?

The three ligaments of the hip joint are the **iliofemoral**, **pubofemoral** and **ischiofemoral** which spiral around the long axis of the femur. The iliofemoral ligament (Y-shaped ligament of Bigelow) is the strongest of the three. The diverging limbs of this ligament attach to the inter-trochanteric line.

What is the blood supply to the femoral head?

The blood supply to the femoral head is mainly from the **trochanteric anastomosis**, from which nutrient vessels run along the neck of the femur to the femoral head. The capsule attaches to the femoral neck and gives off retinacular fibres which are reflected back along the neck to the articular margin of the femoral head and therefore bind down the nutrient vessels to the neck. Hence, a displaced intracapsular fracture of the neck of femur is very likely to sever these vessels and render the head avascular.

There are two other groups of smaller vessels which supply the femoral head. Firstly vessels in the **ligamentum teres** (from the obturator artery) which are important in young children. Secondly, there are some small vessels running up the **medullary canal** into the femoral head.

28. KNEE JOINT

What factors contribute to the stability of the patello-femoral joint?

Three factors control the stability of the patello-femoral joint:

- **Bony stability** is derived from the prominent lateral condyle and deep trochlear groove of the distal femur
- **Ligamentous stability** is derived from the tension of the medial patellar retinaculum
- **Muscular stability** is derived from the oblique insertion of the lowest fibres of vastus medialis. This serves to hold the patella medially during quadriceps contraction.

Where does the capsule of the knee attach?

The capsule is essentially attached to the margins of the articular surfaces of the knee.

The femoral attachment is to the articular margin except at two points. Posteriorly, it is attached to the inter-condylar ridge (a transverse line connecting the postero-superior border of the intercondylar notch). Laterally, the capsule is prolonged to the styloid process of the head of the fibula.

What structures insert onto the inter-condylar area of the tibial plateau?

The inter-condylar area lies between the two articular facets of the tibial plateau. It is divided into anterior and posterior areas.

- The **anterior inter-condylar area** provides attachment for the anterior horns of the medial and lateral menisci to the anterior cruciate ligament
- The **posterior inter-condylar area** provides attachment for the posterior horns of the medial and lateral menisci and to the posterior cruciate ligament

Can you describe the attachments of the cruciate ligaments?

The two cruciate ligaments form a cross in the middle of the knee joint. They are named anterior and posterior with regard to the positions of their attachments on the tibial plateau.

- The origin of the **anterior cruciate** is the anterior inter-condylar area of the tibial plateau. It is inserted into the medial wall of the lateral femoral condyle (i.e. the lateral wall of the femoral inter-condylar notch).
- The origin of the **posterior cruciate** is the posterior inter-condylar area of the tibial plateau. It is inserted into the anterior part of the lateral surface of the medial femoral condyle (i.e. the medial wall of the femoral inter-condylar notch).

What is the clinical sequelae of a ruptured anterior cruciate ligament (ACL)?

The ACL is a very vascular structure and produces an immediate haemarthrosis when ruptured. The function of the ACL is to resist anterior translation of the tibia and internal tibial rotation. ACL rupture will therefore result in the symptoms of instability and giving way.

NB. If the other stabilisers of the knee (ligaments, capsule, menisci and muscles) are strong, these patients may be relatively asymptomatic.

29.   STRUCTURES AROUND THE MEDIAL MALLEOLUS

Can you name the structures behind the medial malleolus?

The structures behind the medial malleolus in order (closest to the malleolus first) are

- Tibialis posterior tendon
- Flexor digitorum longus tendon
- Posterior tibial artery
- Posterior tibial vein
- Posterior tibial nerve
- Flexor hallucis longus tendon

What important structure runs anterior to the medial malleolus?

The long saphenous vein.

What does the posterior tibial nerve supply in the foot?

The posterior tibial nerve provides the **sensory and muscular innervation to the sole of the foot** through its terminal branches, the medial and lateral plantar nerves. There is also a small medial calcaneal branch that supplies the **skin over the heel and some of the medial sole**.

The medial plantar nerve is analogous to the median nerve in the hand. Therefore, it supplies the skin of the sole of the medial 3½ toes, the muscles of the hallux (abductor hallucis, flexor hallucis brevis) except the adductor hallucis and the first lumbrical.

The lateral plantar nerve is analogous to the ulnar nerve in the hand. Therefore it supplies the skin of the sole of the lateral 1½ toes, the interossei, lumbricals 2–4, the muscles of the little toe (flexor digiti minimi brevis, abductor digiti minimi, abductor digiti minimi), the adductor hallucis and flexor digitorum longus.

What other nerves supply the skin of the foot?

The **common peroneal nerve** provides sensation to the dorsum of the foot. The **sural** nerve supplies a small area of skin on the lateral side of the foot. The **saphenous nerve** supplies a small area of skin on the medial side of the foot.

Where does the tibialis posterior tendon insert?

The tibialis posterior tendon inserts into the tuberosity of the navicular bone, all the tarsal bones and the spring ligament.

What is the action of tibialis posterior?

Its action is to plantar flex and invert the foot.

Where does flexor hallucis longus attach?

Flexor hallucis longus arises predominantly from the posterior surface of the fibula. It is the bulkiest and most powerful muscle of the deep calf (it adds 'beef to the heel' during walking).

Flexor hallucis longus inserts into the base of the distal phalanx of the great toe.

What is the action of this muscle?

Its action is to flex the great toe which forms the take off point (the last point to leave the ground) in walking and running.

30.   DERMATOMES OF THE LOWER LIMB

What are the characteristic neurological abnormalities of a L3/4 disc prolapse?

A L3/L4 disc prolapse would cause compression of the L4 nerve root. This would produce a **sensory deficit in the L4 dermatome: postero-lateral thigh, anterior knee and medial leg. Motor weakness** would be seen in the quadriceps muscles and hip adductors, so producing a positive Trendelenburg test. The knee reflex would also be diminished.

What are the characteristic neurological abnormalities of a L4/5 disc prolapse?

A L4/L5 disc prolapse would cause compression of the L5 nerve root. This would produce a **sensory deficit in the L5 dermatome: antero-lateral leg, dorsum of the foot and the great toe. Motor weakness** would be seen in extensor hallucis longus, gluteus medius and extensor digitorum longus and brevis, so producing weakness of dorsiflexion of the foot and toes and a positive Trendelenburg test.

What are the characteristic neurological abnormalities of L5/S1 disc prolapse?

A L5/S1 disc prolapse would cause compression of the S1 nerve root. This would produce a **sensory deficit in the S1 dermatome: lateral foot, heel and web spaces of the 4th and 5th toes. Motor weakness** would be seen in the peroneus longus and brevis (weak foot eversion), gastrocnemius-soleus complex (weakness of foot plantar flexion i.e. standing on tiptoes) and gluteus maximus. The ankle reflex would also be diminished.

What are the effects of a central lumbar disc prolapse?

A large mid-line disc herniation may compress several roots of the cauda equina causing the **Cauda Equina Syndrome**, so leading to back and perianal pain. There may also be difficulty in voiding, increased urinary frequency or overflow incontinence, faecal incontinence may also be seen. Patients may complain of numbness of both feet and difficulty in walking. Urgent MRI and surgery is required.

What are the common causes of a common peroneal nerve palsy?

The causes may be divided into iatrogenic and non-iatrogenic.

Iatrogenic causes include nerve compression secondary to poor patient positioning during an operation or accidental division of the nerve during an operation. Nerve compression may occur when the patient is in the Lloyd Davies position during a urological or anorectal procedure. Another common cause is nerve compression from a tight Plaster of Paris.

Non-iatrogenic causes include trauma and compression secondary to a tumour.

What are the effects of a common peroneal nerve palsy?

A common peroneal palsy produces both **motor and sensory deficits**. The motor deficit causes peroneal (through superficial branch) and anterior tibial (through deep branch) muscle weakness, thus producing a foot drop. Sensation is lost over the dorsum of the foot and lateral leg.

What is meralgia paraesthetica?

Meralgia paraesthetica is compression of the lateral cutaneous nerve of the thigh (L2–L3) on the lateral aspect of the anterior superior iliac spine. This produces numbness and paraesthesia over the antero-lateral aspect of the thigh.

31.   CARPAL TUNNEL DECOMPRESSION

Can you describe where you would place your incision for a carpal tunnel decompression?

A skin incision would be placed in the palm along the proximal curved skin crease that lies at the base of the thenar eminence (the 'life or longevity' line). This usually corresponds to the radial border of the ring finger. The proximal limit of the incision should be the transverse flexor skin crease of the wrist.

What structures will be visible after the skin has been incised?

Immediately below the skin is fat. Below this is flexor retinaculum and palmaris longus proximally, (absent in approximately 10% of cases) and the palmar aponeurosis distally. Abductor pollicus brevis may be seen medially.

How would you normally proceed with the operation?

The incision is deepened through the palmar aponeurosis and distal end of the flexor retinaculum to reveal the median nerve. It is important to remain on the ulnar side of the median nerve and the palmaris longus tendon (if present) to avoid damaging the muscular branch of the median nerve (recurrent motor branch that supplies the thenar eminence muscles).

A MacDonald's dissector is passed underneath the retinaculum to guide the proximal and distal release.

How do you differentiate the median nerve from the flexor tendons?

The median nerve is differentiated from the surrounding tendons because it is usually whiter and has fine vessels visible on its surface.

How would you minimise sensory loss over the thenar eminence?

Sensory loss over the thenar eminence is minimised if an incision is placed on the ulnar side of the median nerve. This would preserve the palmar branch of the median nerve, which supplies the skin over the thenar eminence.

What is the importance of hypothyroidism and carpal tunnel syndrome?

Hypothyroidism is a cause of carpal tunnel syndrome. If the hypothyroidism is adequately treated, symptoms of carpal tunnel syndrome should regress. Therefore, one should not perform carpal tunnel decompression in patients with untreated hypothyroidism.

32.   RIGHT HEMICOLECTOMY

How would you prepare a patient for a right hemicolectomy who has already been staged?

The pre-operative preparation involves identification of any co-existing cardio-respiratory disease which may compromise the anaesthesia. A chest X-ray and ECG should be performed in the pre-operative work-up, in addition to performing base-line blood investigations including full blood count, urea and electrolytes and glucose. It is prudent to group and save the patient. Informed consent must be obtained from the patient.

No bowel preparation is required but DVT prophylaxis should be instituted. Subcutaneous tinzaparin peri- and post-operatively together with thrombo-embolic deterrent stockings (TEDS) is prescribed.

How do you perform a right hemicolectomy?

Having placed the patient in the supine position and under a general anaesthetic, I would make a mid-line incision (alternatively transverse).

A full laparotomy is performed to exclude any co-existing intra-abdominal pathology.

The tumour is identified (the tumour should be minimally handled). The caecum and ascending colon are drawn medially. Dissection of the parietal peritoneum is carried out to dissect the right colon from the posterior abdominal wall. It is important to identify the right ureter, gonadal vessels and duodenum as injury to these structures may occur.

The hepatic flexure is immobilised and any ileal bands may be divided so that the whole of the right colon can be lifted from the abdomen.

The mesenteric vessels are identified and the ileocolic artery and vein divided. The right colic and the right branch of the middle colic vessels are also divided. The extent of resection depends on the site and size of the tumour but includes approximately 25 cm of terminal ileum to the middle third of the transverse colon. The right half of the greater omentum is removed en bloc. Having removed and excised the specimen, the divided ends of the ileum and colon are cleaned with aqueous iodine solution.

An end to end anastomosis is performed using 3-O Vicryl suture using an interrupted sero submucosal technique. The mesenteric window is closed using 2-O Vicryl.

How do you close your mid-line abdominal incision?

The mid-line abdominal incision is closed with a loop nylon suture which is at least four times the length of the wound (Jenkin's rule). The closure technique involves taking 1 cm bites, 1 cm apart ensuring that the anterior fascial layer of the rectal sheath is taken. The skin is closed with staples.

Do you usually use an abdominal drain?

No, I do not routinely place a drain following this operation.

33.   PNEUMOPERITONEUM

What is the commonest cause of free intra-abdominal gas?

The commonest cause of free intra-peritoneal gas is a perforated peptic ulcer.

What proportion of perforated ulcers do not demonstrate any free intra-abdominal gas?

Approximately 10%.

How much free gas needs to be present to be detected on erect chest X-ray?

1 ml of free gas can be detected.

What are the other common causes of perforation?

Perforation of a colonic diverticulum, appendix and a malignant colonic tumour are the other common causes.

What conditions may mimic the appearance of a pneumoperitoneum?

These include the presence of intestine (colon) between the liver and the diaphragm (Chilaiditi's syndrome), subphrenic abscess, pulmonary collapse, sub-diaphragmatic fat and cysts in pneumatosis intestinalis.

What can you see on this plain abdominal X-ray?

Calcification can be seen in the wall of a large aortic aneurysm.

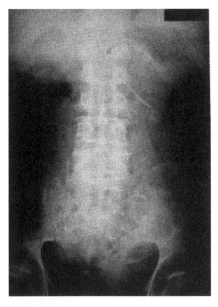

What are the X-ray features of a leaking abdominal aortic aneurysm?

The signs include

- Soft tissue retro-peritoneal mass
- Loss of the psoas outline
- Loss of the renal outline
- Displacement of the kidney

34.   FEMORAL HERNIA REPAIR

What approaches are there to a femoral hernia repair?

Femoral hernias may be repaired using a variety of approaches, namely the **low approach** (Lockwood), **high approach** (Lotheissen) and the **extra-peritoneal approach** (McEvedy's).

When might you use each of these approaches?

The **low approach** is predominantly used for elective operations.

The **high approach** has the advantage that one can repair co-existing inguinal and femoral hernia, but suffers from the disadvantage that it damages the inguinal canal and could lead to a subsequent inguinal hernia.

The **McEvedy approach** is probably the best for suspected strangulated hernias as it provides excellent access for assessment of the bowel and subsequent bowel resection if necessary.

Can you describe how you would actually carry out a femoral hernia repair using the low approach?

With full informed consent, the patient is placed in the supine position. The anaesthetic may be general or local.

An incision is made in the crease of the groin below the medial half of the inguinal ligament. Having dissected down through the superficial tissues over the hernia, the hernial sac is exposed and clear identification of the sac is made. The sac is cautiously incised. The external fat is swept away to expose the neck which lies between the inguinal ligament anteriorly and the pectineal ligament posteriorly. Having noted the position of the femoral vein which lies just laterally, the sac is emptied and transfixed and ligated with 2-O Vicryl. The sac is excised 1 cm distal to the ligature. Next the defect is closed by apposing the inguinal and pectineal ligaments with a non-absorbable suture such as 2-O Ethibond or nylon. Care is taken not to injure or constrict the femoral vein when the ligature is tied.

An alternative method of repair is to fill the femoral canal with a plug of rolled mesh which may be secured with sutures. The subcutaneous tissues and skin are then closed with 3-O Vicryl.

During your operation, you suspect that the femoral hernia contains strangulated bowel, what is your course of management?

If one encounters a strangulated hernia when performing a low approach one should have no hesitation to open the abdomen formally and inspect to confirm bowel viability.

What features would suggest that the bowel is non-viable?

Non-viable bowel is green, black or purple, has no sheen or pulsation in the mesenteric vessels and is malodorous.

35.   POSITIONING OF THE SURGICAL PATIENT

What cardiorespiratory changes occur when a patient is placed in the supine position?

When placed in the supine position, stroke volume and cardiac output increase as a result of increase in central venous pressure. A bradycardia may be seen as baroreceptors sense the increase in arterial pressure so leading to a fall in heart rate and systemic vascular resistance.

Respiratory changes may also be seen and include changes in the ventilation and perfusion ratio, which becomes more uniform. Hence, the dependent portions of the lungs are better perfused as a result of gravity.

What nerves may be injured as a result of direct pressure during anaesthesia?

Peripheral nerves may be damaged via local ischaemia caused by compression or stretching. It is most likely to occur in extreme positions and prolonged surgery.

The **ulnar nerve** may be injured and this is the most common nerve injury occurring during anaesthesia. Compression occurs between the medial epicondyle, the humerus and the edge of the operating table.

The **radial nerve** too may be injured due to compression between the edge of the operating table or arm board and the shaft of the humerus.

The **brachial plexus** may also be injured during stretching, especially when the arm is abducted to more than 90°.

The **facial nerve** may be injured through compression by the anaesthetist's fingers against the ramus of the mandible or by a face mask.

The **supra-orbital nerve** may also be damaged by compression, for example by tracheal tube connectors. Other nerve injuries include damage to the sciatic by direct compression if the patient is undergoing prolonged surgery.

The **common peroneal nerve** may be injured particularly in the Lloyd Davis or lithotomy positions.

When might you use the Trendelenburg (head down) position?

The Trendelenburg position might be used when performing pelvic surgery or during insertion of central venous lines.

What are the physiological effects of the Trendelenburg position?

The physiological effects include a rise in the central venous pressure with a concomitant increase in cardiac output. Prolonged head down position might cause venous congestion and oedema in the head and neck.

In addition, there is a greater reduction in the functional residual capacity as a result of pressure of the abdominal contents on the diaphragm.

When would you use the lithotomy position?

The lithotomy position may be used for operations on the perineum, anus, rectum and for urological procedures.

Why is it important to carefully position a patient in lithotomy?

Careful positioning is needed as **hip dislocation** can occur if there is slippage of the lithotomy poles. **Compartment syndrome** has been described and is thought to be caused by pressure on the calf muscles by the stirrup poles. Back-ache is common and the sacrum must be supported and not hang over the end of the table. Marked flexion of the hips and knees may also cause **sacro-iliac strain**.

What nerves may be injured when a patient is placed in lithotomy position?

Nerve injuries can occur in the lithotomy position and these include injuries to the tibial, femoral, obturator, common peroneal, sciatic and saphenous nerves.

Do all these nerve injuries lead to permanent disability?

Neuropraxia is the most common form of nerve injury and complete clinical recovery usually occurs within 6–8 weeks. However, it may take several months. Severe damage may be associated with permanent injury.

36. SURGICAL DIATHERMY

What types of diathermy do you know?

There are two basic varieties of surgical diathermy – **unipolar** and **bipolar**. **Unipolar (or monopolar) diathermy** is the type most commonly used. It involves using a large surface electrode which is the patient plate and an active electrode with a very small surface area of contact (which the operating surgeon uses) which concentrates a powerful current to the tip so producing heat at the point of operative contact.

Bipolar diathermy is used when performing delicate procedures as in neurosurgery, ophthalmic surgery, plastic surgery and micro-surgery. It consists of two electrodes combined in one unit, namely the diathermy forceps. This results in a flow of current through which the tissue is gripped. The forceps ends are active and heating occurs in the tissue held in between the forceps.

What advantage does bipolar diathermy have over monopolar diathermy?

Bipolar diathermy has greater accuracy and safety compared with unipolar diathermy. This results in reduced tissue damage.

What other effects apart from coagulation does diathermy have?

Diathermy may be used for **fulguration** and **cutting**. In fulguration, a high intensity current is passed through the tissue causing extensive coagulation and necrosis. This may be used for coagulating as well as destroying small growths in the bladder and rectum for example.

In cutting diathermy, an electric arc is used to incise the tissue and cauterise the divided surfaces. This effect is produced when a smooth sine wave is passed through the tissue producing a very hot cutting arc and relatively bloodless field.

What are the complications of diathermy?

Complications include an explosion if there are any flammable or volatile anaesthetic agents being used (for example ether or cyclopropane).

Explosion:	Gas explosion in obstructed hollow viscera
Electrocution:	Electrocution of the patient or the surgeon, if there are faulty cables
Burns:	Superficial burns if an inflammable spirit is used, for example if there is pooling in the umbilicus
	Diathermy burns due to improper application of the indifferent electrode or if there is a break in the connection to the diathermy unit or if there is accidental activation of the foot pedal or contact with electrode active retractors

	Inadvertent diathermy burns are also a particular hazard of laparoscopic surgery
Channeling:	Channelling effects may occur whereby heat is produced where the current tends to be at its greatest, leading to thrombosis of a vessel with a narrow pedicle, so causing ischaemic damage of that organ, for example in operations of the penis or testis.
Coupling:	The phenomenon of direct coupling whereby instrument contact occurs whilst the diathermy is activated
	Capacitor coupling and retained heat in the diathermy tip are other complications unique to laparoscopic surgery

37.   APPENDICECTOMY

Can you tell me how you would prepare a patient for appendicectomy?

Having taken a full history and examination and identified any anaesthetic risks, informed consent would then be obtained. Pre-operative antibiotics would be given, consisting of 1 gram of metronidazole per rectum or 500 mg intravenously.

Why do you give antibiotics?

The incidence of wound and intra-abdominal infections is high following appendicitis and prophylactic antibiotics should be routinely given.

What incision would you use?

A Lanz incision.

Where do you make this excision?

I would start the incision 2 cm below and medial to the right anterior superior iliac spine and extend it medially for approximately 4 cm.

Can you describe how you would perform an appendicectomy?

Having incised the skin, the subcutaneous fat and Scarpa's fascia, the external oblique aponeurosis is incised in line with its fibres. This exposes the muscular fibres of the internal oblique which run at right angles. The internal oblique and transversus abdominal muscles are split using straight Mayo scissors. The fold of peritoneum is then picked up and an incision is made with a knife. The hole is enlarged with scissors in line with the skin incision. The next step involves taking a specimen of peritoneal fluid for microbiological culture. Once in the peritoneal cavity the caecum is located and followed distally to find the base of the appendix.

If you find that the appendix is not inflamed, what would you do next?

I would examine the tip of the appendix to exclude a carcinoid tumour and also examine the caecum looking for inflammation or carcinoma. I would also inspect the distal 1.5 m of the ileum and its mesentery to exclude Crohn's disease and a Meckel's diverticulum. I would also look for mesenteric adenitis and examine the bladder, right iliac vessels, right inguinal orifices, the liver, gall bladder, ascending colon and in the female the right ovary, fallopian tube and uterus.
Perform an appendicectomy.

Do you bury the appendix stump?

No, I do not routinely bury the appendix stump with a purse string, though it is well described technique.

How would you manage an appendix mass?

An appendix mass can be treated conservatively. However, it is important to carefully monitor the patient's clinical state. Indications for surgical intervention

- The mass becomes tender or enlarges
- The patient becomes toxic with a swinging pyrexia, tachycardia and increasing white cell count
- The patient develops features of generalised peritonitis, obstruction or paralytic ileus.

38. LAPAROSCOPIC CHOLECYSTECTOMY

What proportion of cholecystectomies are performed laparoscopically in the UK?

90%

Are there any absolute contra-indications to laparoscopic cholecystectomy?

The only absolute contra-indication is a bleeding diathesis.

How do you create a pneumoperitoneum?

I would create a pneumoperitoneum with an open technique using a Hasson cannula. Having confirmed and successfully entered the peritoneal cavity I would insufflate with carbon dioxide.

Why do you not use a Veress needle to create a pneumoperitoneum?

The Veress needle technique is a blind procedure and is associated with a higher incidence of visceral injury, though it is a well described and acceptable technique.

What is special about the Veress needle?

It is a spring loaded needle with a blunt tip.

What inflation pressure do you usually set to maintain your pneumoperitoneum?

This varies according to the body habitus of the patient but a pressure of 12 mmHg is normally adequate.

What is the danger of using excessively high intra-abdominal insufflation pressure?

The dangers include development of respiratory and cardiovascular problems. With elevated intra-abdominal pressures, there may be splinting of the diaphragm and impairment of gaseous exchange. As a result, higher inflation pressures are used by the anaesthetist which further increases the risk of spontaneous pneumothorax. The high intra-thoracic pressure also reduces venous return and preload to the heart, leading to a fall in cardiac output. High intra-abdominal pressure also impedes venous return from the lower limbs, and may increase the risk of DVT.

How many ports do you use for a laparoscopic cholecystectomy?

I routinely use 4 ports, but it may successfully be performed using 3.

What must you identify during the operation, in order to minimise the risk of bile duct injury?

Calot's triangle. You must demonstrate what you believe to be the cystic duct is actually continuous with the gall bladder.

What is Calot's triangle?   Calot's triangle is formed by the cystic duct, common hepatic duct and the liver edge.

What lies in Calot's triangle?   The cystic artery.

What structure is commonly encountered adjacent to the artery?   A lymph node.

What is the cystic artery usually a branch of?   The right hepatic artery.

39.   EMERGENCY TRACHEOSTOMY

What are the indications for tracheostomy?

The indications for tracheostomy include conditions

- Causing an upper airway obstruction
- Necessitating protection of the tracheo-bronchial tree
- Causing a respiratory failure

These include

- Congenital disorders such as laryngeal webs and subglottic/upper tracheal stenosis
- Trauma
- Radiotherapy
- Prolonged endo-tracheal intubation
- Infections such as acute epiglottitis, Ludwig's angina, diphtheria
- Malignant tumours
- Bilateral laryngeal paralysis
- Protection of the tracheobronchial tree
- Neurological conditions such as multiple sclerosis, myasthenia gravis
- Trauma due to head injury/multiple facial fractures
- Conditions causing respiratory failure
- Removal of bronchial secretions

How would you perform an emergency tracheostomy?

With the patient in a supine position and the head held in a central but extended position (a sand bag is placed beneath the shoulders), a vertical incision is made from the lower border of the thyroid cartilage in the mid-line to the supra-sternal notch. The incision is then deepened and extended between the strap muscles. The thyroid isthmus is divided to expose the anterior trachea. The trachea is incised vertically through the second, third and fourth rings. A tracheal dilator is inserted to secure an airway and a tracheostomy tube introduced.

40. TONSILLECTOMY

Can you describe the anatomical relations of the tonsil?

The tonsil is a large collection of lymphatic tissue projecting into the oropharynx from the tonsillar fossa. It lies between the palatopharyngeal and palatoglossal folds, the palatoglossal fold being anterior. The tonsil extends up into the soft palate and downwards onto the dorsum of the tongue. The superior constrictor muscle lies laterally.

What is the relation of the facial artery to the tonsil?

The facial artery and two of its branches (ascending palatine and tonsillar) lie lateral to the tonsil with the superior constrictor and pharyngeal submucosa in between.

Is the internal carotid artery in danger at tonsillectomy?

No, the internal carotid artery lies approximately 2.5 cm postero-laterally and is separated from the pharyngeal wall by loose fat and connective tissue.

What is the blood supply to the tonsil?

The main blood supply is from the tonsillar branch of the facial artery. There are smaller contributions from the lingual, ascending palatine and pharyngeal arteries.

What vessel is most commonly associated with venous haemorrhage after tonsillectomy?

The external palatine (paratonsillar) vein is the most common cause of venous haemorrhage after tonsillectomy.

During an attack of tonsillitis, which group of lymph nodes are usually affected?

The deep cervical group including the jugulo-digastric group below the angle of the mandible.

What are the indications for tonsillectomy?

- Recurrent attacks of tonsillitis (4 attacks per year)
- Following quinsy
- Tonsillar hypertrophy causing airway obstruction
- Recurrent tonsillitis associated with complications such as acute or chronic otitis media
- Suspected malignancy

What are the complications of tonsillectomy?

Immediate complications

- Intra-op haemorrhage
  Clot into upper airway.

Early complications

- Infection
- Otitis media
- Reactionary haemorrhage (occurs within a few hours)

Late complications

- Secondary haemorrhage (1% cases) occurring between the 5th and 8th post-operative days – due to infection
- Pulmonary complications (rare) including pneumonia

How would you manage a reactionary haemorrhage?

Reactionary haemorrhage must be dealt with as an emergency. One should proceed through the normal protocol of establishing and maintaining an airway, breathing and circulation. Blood should be taken for cross-match and the patient urgently prepared for theatre. The bleeding points should be identified, cauterised or ligated as appropriate.

CLINICAL PATHOLOGY AND PRINCIPLES OF SURGERY

1. Acute and chronic inflammation
2. Granulomas
3. Thrombophilia
4. Atherosclerosis
5. Wound healing
6. Ascites
7. Pancreatitis
8. Asbestos
9. Amyloid
10. Gram staining
11. Blood transfusion
12. Surgical consent
13. Diabetes in surgery
14. Post-operative analgesia
15. Screening and surgery
16. Stoma
17. Malignant myeloma
18. HIV infection
19. Urinary tract calculi
20. Intestinal fistulae
21. Alcohol
22. Infantile hypertrophic pyloric stenosis
23. Leg ulcers
24. Lung carcinoma
25. Transurethral (TUR) syndrome
26. Colorectal cancer
27. Nipple discharge
28. Ulcerative colitis
29. Varicose veins
30. Hypertension

1.   ACUTE AND CHRONIC INFLAMMATION

How would you define acute inflammation?

Acute inflammation is the biological response to injury. It consists of

- Activation of plasma enzyme systems (complement, kinins and clotting)
- Stimulation of cells resident in the tissue (mast cells and macrophages)
- Recruitment of circulating cells

What are the five cardinal signs of inflammation?

- **Erythema** due to dilatation of the blood vessels
- **Heat** due to the increased blood flow
- **Swelling** due to the accumulation of fluid and proteins
- **Pain** due to swelling of the tissues and direct stimulation of sensory neural afferents by the inflammatory mediators (such as Substance P, Nerve Growth Factor)
- **Loss of function** due to the pain and swelling

What are the phases of acute inflammation?

There are three phases

- **Vascular phase**: hyperaemia and increased vascular permeability
- **Cellular phase**: initial migration of leucocytes and subsequently macrophages
- **Resolution phase**

What is the eventual outcome of acute inflammation?

The eventual outcome of acute inflammation is healing by resolution, regeneration or repair.

Can you name the important groups of inflammatory mediators involved in acute inflammation?

- **Plasma derived chemotactic agents** (complement, kinins, fibrinolytic system)
- **Cell derived chemotactic agents** (bacterial products, platelet activating factor, tumour necrosis factor)
- **Vascular permeability factors** (histamine, kinins, leukotrienes, complement)
- **Vasodilators** (kinins, histamine, prostaglandins)

What is the definition of chronic inflammation?

Clinically, chronic inflammation may be defined as inflammation present for weeks or months.
Histologically, chronic inflammation may be defined as inflammation that occurs simultaneously with attempted healing.

What are the causes of chronic inflammation?

The causes of chronic inflammation may be divided into processes persisting following acute inflammation or processes starting de novo. In both these instances there is minimal acute inflammation but a large accumulation of macrophages, lymphocytes and plasma cells.

What are the main histological features of chronic inflammation?

The main histological features are

- Monocyte and macrophage infiltration
- Fibrin deposition
- Endarteritis obliterans
- Presence of lymphocytes and plasma cells
- Fibrosis and tissue destruction present (e.g. polymorphonuclear leucocytes and eosinophils)

2.   GRANULOMAS

What is a granuloma?

A granuloma is a **chronic inflammatory reaction** containing predominantly a collection of cells of the **mononuclear phagocyte** series arranged in a compact mass.

What conditions are associated with granuloma formulation?

The conditions can be broadly divided into

- **Indigestible organisms** (e.g. TB, leprosy, syphilis, schistosomiasis)
- **Foreign bodies** (e.g. silica)
- **Idiopathic** (sarcoidosis)
- **Crohn's disease**

How does a tuberculous granuloma differ from other types of granuloma?

In a tubercle follicle there is **central caseous necrosis** surrounded by a zone of epithelioid cells. Macrophages fuse together to form giant cells whose nuclei are arranged around the periphery of the cell, forming a horseshoe or ring: **Langhan's giant cell**.

What are giant cells?

Giant cells are formed when macrophages encounter insoluble material and coalesce with one another. Thus, giant cells may be seen around foreign bodies e.g. talc, keratin, silica, suture material.

Can you name some specific types of giant cells?

- Foreign body giant cells
- Touton giant cells (classically in xanthoma)
- Langhan's giant cell

3.   THROMBOPHILIA

What is Virchow's triad?

Virchow's triad refers to three factors that are involved in the pathogenesis of thrombosis.

- **Vessel wall**
- **Flow of blood**
- **Constituents of the blood**

Derangements of any of these factors determine the occurrence of thrombosis.

Can you describe the stages of development of a venous thrombosis?

The development of a venous thrombosis consists of five stages:

- **Primary platelet thrombus**
Platelets adhere to vein wall forming a 'pale' thrombus.

- **Coralline thrombus**
Fibrin deposition and thrombin formation encourages further platelet accumulation. A laminated thrombus forms (alternate layers of platelets and fibrin with entrapped red blood cells = lines of Zahn).

- **Occluding thrombus**
Growth of corralline thrombus leads to occlusion of the vein lumen: 'red thrombus'.

- **Consecutive clot**
The stationary column of blood beyond the occluding thrombus clots to form a consecutive clot which extends up to the next venous tributary.

- **Propagated clot**
The clot may propagate or be endothelialised. Propagation is a complex process whereby further thrombus develops and extends up the vein. The clot may lie loose in the vein attached only at one point or be well anchored.

What are the main risk factors for DVT?

The main risk factors for DVT include

Surgical related factors

- Pelvic, hip or lower limb fracture
- Pelvic and lower limb surgery
- Prolonged major surgery (including lower limb amputation)

Patient related factors

- Malignancy
- Hypercoagulable state
- Previous thromboembolic disease
- Immobility
- Age (>40 years)
- Pregnancy
- Co-existing illness (CVA, heart failure, MI)

Can you suggest a DVT prophylaxis regimen?

A suitable prophylactic regimen depends on the DVT risk of the patient.

Low risk patients
- early mobilisation

Moderate risk patients
- TEDS (calf length)
- Tinzaparin 3500 iu s/c od or Heparin 5000 iu s/c bd
- Continue regimen until full mobilisation

High risk patients
- TEDS
- Tinzaparin 3500 iu s/c or Heparin 5000 iu s/c tds
- +/- Intra-operative pneumatic calf compression devices
- Continue regimen until full mobilisation
  (Aspirin is used by orthopaedic surgeons.)

What are the potential complications of DVT?

Systemic complications

- Pulmonary embolism
- Pulmonary hypertension

Local complications

- Venous gangrene (rare complication of massive iliofemoral thrombosis)
- Post-phlebitic limb

What inherited conditions are associated with thrombophilia?

- Anti-thrombin III deficiency
- Protein S deficiency
- Protein C deficiency
- Factor V Leiden (mutations causing resistance to activated protein C)
- $\alpha2$ macroglobulin
- Klippel Trenaunay syndrome

What acquired conditions cause blood hyper-coagulability?

These may be divided into physiological, disease and drug related.

Physiological

- Pregnancy
- Obesity

Disease related

- Malignancy
- Past history of DVT or PE
- Congestive cardiac failure
- Lupus anticoagulant
- Varicose veins

Drug induced

- Oral contraceptive pill
- Hormone replacement therapy

4.   ATHEROSCLEROSIS

What do you understand by the term atherosclerosis?

Atherosclerosis is the **focal intimal thickening** of medium and large sized arteries, secondary to the accumulation of lipids, fibrous tissue and smooth muscle proliferation.

Can you describe the pathogenesis of an atherosclerotic plaque?

The process of atherosclerosis commences in a normal vessel and then progresses through the stages of **fatty streak → fibrous plaque → complicated lesion** with **calcification**, **haemorrhage**, **ulceration** and **thrombosis**.

The process is thought to begin with **endothelial cell dysfunction**. Biochemical (hyperlipidaemia) and haemodynamic (hypertension) stresses serve to increase endothelial cell permeability. The accumulation of lipid in the arterial wall damages the endothelium further, and exposes the subendothelial tissue. This in turn encourages **platelet adherence** and **smooth muscle proliferation**.

What is the role of macrophages in atherosclerosis?

The macrophage is an important cellular component in atherosclerosis as it transports lipid into vessel walls, secretes growth factors for smooth muscle and endothelial cells, and produces oxygen free radicals.

What are the complications of atherosclerosis?

Complications occur through weakening of the arterial wall or narrowing of the arterial lumen.

Weakening of the arterial wall may cause aneurysm formation. Aneurysms in turn may produce complications through local pressure effects, rupture, thrombosis or distal infarction as a result of embolisation. In rare instances, thrombosis in an aneurysm may produce distal ischaemia due to a narrowing of the lumen.

Narrowing of the arterial lumen can lead to distal sequelae. The lumen may be stenosed or occluded so causing distal ischaemia, the severity of which is dependent on the collateral blood supply. If the vessel is an end artery, as in the coronary arteries, infarction will occur. Narrowing may also produce embolic phenomena with consequent distal infarction.

Plaque rupture

What is the difference between a true and a false aneurysm?

A **true aneurysm** is a permanent, irreversible localised dilatation of an artery. *All arterial layers.*

A **false aneurysm** is formed when there is leakage of blood from the vessel with a resultant perivascular haematoma which communicates with the vessel lumen. It is termed a 'false' aneurysm because it is not lined with vascular endothelium.

How might you classify aneurysms?

Aneurysms may be classified according to their morphology (fusiform and saccular) or aetiology into atherosclerotic, infective, dissecting, traumatic and congenital.

5.   WOUND HEALING

Can you describe the phases of wound healing by primary intention?

Cleanly incised wounds (where the edges are in close apposition) heal by primary intention. The phases of wound healing are

- Initial haematoma formation
- 2–3 hours later an acute inflammatory reaction occurs with subsequent epidermal cell migration from the skin edges
- At 12 hours, epidermal cells proliferate from the basal layer of the epidermis
- At 48 hours, macrophage migration into the inflammatory infiltrate in the dermis serves to co-ordinate further healing
- By day 3–4 fibroblast infiltration occurs. Collagen and other tissue proteins are synthesised.
- By day 6, collagen bundles cross the wound
- Further macrophage and fibroblast infiltration occurs accompanied by neovascularisation
- Weeks later the scar is still slightly hyperaemic, with good fibrous union
- By 6 months, 70% of the tensile strength of the wound has been achieved
- At 1 year the scar is mature and appears pale

What are the main histological differences between healing by primary and secondary intention?

In contrast to healing by primary intention, healing by secondary intention occurs in open wounds (e.g. following a burn, necrosis or infection). Similar cellular processes occur in both these types of healing. However, there are some important differences.

- Formation of neovascularised collagen producing tissue (granulation tissue) is much greater in wounds healing by secondary intention, because the size of the defect is much larger
- Within the first week, myofibroblasts appear at the edge of a wound healing by secondary intention. The size of the defect is thus reduced both by wound contracture as well as epidermal cell migration and proliferation.
- Wounds healing by secondary intention frequently have a thick collagenous scar in the dermis due to the non-apposed epidermal layer

What factors affect wound healing?

The factors affecting wound healing may be divided into local and systemic:

Local factors include

- Foreign body
- Haematoma
- Infection
- Poor blood supply

Systemic factors include

- Malnutrition (lack of vitamin C, zinc and certain amino acids)
- Drugs (steroids and immunosuppressive agents impair wound healing)
- Jaundice
- Alcoholic cirrhosis
- Radiotherapy   *Diabetes. Cushing's.*

Can you describe some technical measures that may help optimise tissue healing in a patient undergoing operation?

These measures can be classified into operative and non-operative.

The **non-operative measures** include reducing infection by using prophylactic antibiotics, laminar air flow and reducing the number of non-essential personnel in theatres.

Operative measures include gentle handling of tissues, short operation time and irrigation/lavage of dirty wounds.

What is abdominal wound dehiscence?

Abdominal wound dehiscence occurs when the fascial layer of the abdomen is not intact. In the majority of cases it represents a technical surgical error. It is important to exclude an intra-abdominal problem as the cause of the dehiscence. Abdominal lavage, wound irrigation and re-suturing forms the mainstay of treatment.

How is abdominal dehiscence managed?

Abdominal dehiscence is managed by aggressive resuscitation and preparation of the patient for theatre and re-suture. In certain extenuating circumstances (e.g. chronic intra-abdominal sepsis) dehiscences may be left open allowing sepsis to drain.

6.   ASCITES

What is ascites?

Ascites is an **abnormal interstitial fluid accumulation in the peritoneal cavity**.

Can you outline how ascites is formed?

Fluid accumulation within the peritoneal cavity is dependent on regulating the inflow and outflow of fluid. The most important factors are the inflow pressure, capillary permeability, colloid osmotic pressure and lymphatic outflow capacity.

The inflow of fluid is controlled by venous pressure. A pressure gradient exists for peritoneal fluid absorption which is created by negative intrathoracic pressure generated during the respiratory cycle. The outflow fluid is controlled primarily by lymphatics which are concentrated in the subdiaphragmatic region of the right upper quadrant and muscular portion of the diaphragm.

When there is an imbalance of fluid movements, ascites may form.

How do you classify ascites?

Ascites may be classified in a number of ways. One method is to divide it descriptively into cirrhotic, malignant, pancreatic and chylous forms. Another is to divide it into transudate and exudate causes.

Based on your understanding, how might liver cirrhosis cause ascites?

Cirrhosis produces ascites by increasing both portal vascular resistance and splanchnic blood flow. These two factors act together to produce portal hypertension, which in turn leads to increased visceral lymph formation. This resultant increase in lymph production exceeds absorption capacity, thus fluid accumulates in the peritoneal space and the volume of extracellular fluid falls. The kidney responds to this fall in extracellular fluid volume by stimulating the renin-aldosterone axis leading to an increase in extracellular fluid volume. This in turn causes further stimulation of lymph formation and exacerbates the ascites.

What tumours are particularly associated with malignant ascites?

Ovary, breast, colon, pancreas, stomach, liver and lymphoma.

7.   PANCREATITIS

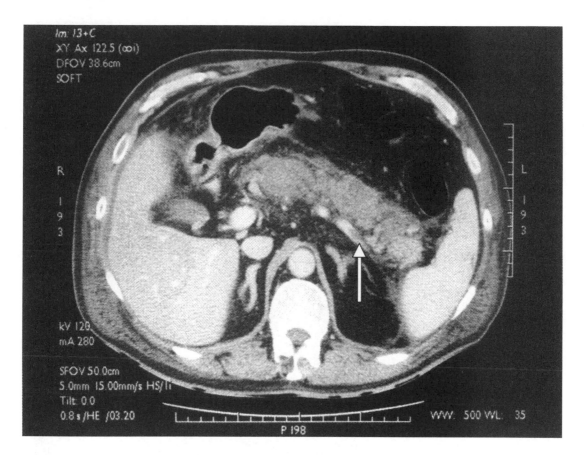

Does the pancreas look normal?	No. The pancreas is swollen and enlarged. There is also evidence of fat stranding.
What do you think is the likely underlying pathology	Acute pancreatitis.
Can you see any known complication of acute pancreatitis on the CT scan?	There is evidence of splenic vein thrombosis (white arrow).

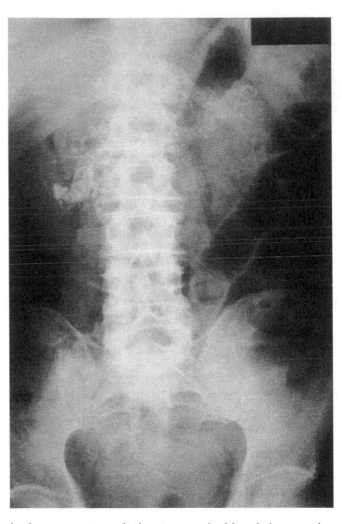

What can you see on this plain abdominal X-ray?

Marked pancreatic calcification and dilated loops of small bowel.

What is acute pancreatitis?

Acute pancreatitis is acute inflammation in the pancreas heralded by the acute onset of abdominal pain, accompanied by increased level of pancreatic enzymes in the blood or urine or both. In mild acute pancreatitis there is peri-pancreatic fat necrosis but no pancreatic necrosis. In severe acute pancreatitis, there is extensive pancreatic necrosis and haemorrhage.

How common is acute pancreatitis?

The incidence is between 5–11:100,000 population. It usually affects adults between 30 and 70 years old. Men and women are affected equally.

Can you name the main causes of acute pancreatitis?

The factors most commonly associated with acute pancreatitis are **gallstones** and **alcohol** abuse. These account for approximately 80% of cases. The remaining causes include **idiopathic** (the next largest group), trauma (including ERCP), **infections** (mumps, Coxsackie), **drugs** (such as thiazide diuretics, steroids), **congenital** (pancreatic divisum) **metabolic** disorders (hyperlipidaemia) and **endocrine** disorders (hyperparathyroidism).

What is the pathogenesis of acute pancreatitis?

The pancreas synthesises enzymes including proteases and lipases that are normally activated in the duodenum. However, in pancreatitis the digestive enzymes are activated within the pancreas and autodigestion occurs. It is unclear how this actually occurs. There appear to be two major forms of the disease depending on where the enzymes become activated. The mild form results from activation in the cytoplasm of the acinar cells causing limited cell injury. The severe form results from activation within the parenchyma of the gland causing more widespread injury.

In acute severe pancreatitis there may be haemorrhage with areas of grey-white necrotic softening, leading to areas of white fat necrosis. The acute inflammatory response around the areas of necrosis may become secondarily infected and form abscesses. Liquefied areas are walled off to form pseudocysts of varying sizes.

What is chronic pancreatitis?

Chronic pancreatitis is a persistent, usually progressive, inflammation of the pancreas causing sclerosis and destruction of the parenchyma. Clinically, it is associated with recurrent episodes of abdominal pain but may be present without pain. Both endocrine and exocrine functions may be impaired.

What is the incidence of chronic pancreatitis?

Its incidence is 3:100,000 population. It is more common in males than females. The average age of onset is 40 years old. In industrialised countries the commonest cause is excess alcohol ingestion (>75% of cases). Other causes are recurrent attacks of acute pancreatitis and uncommonly obstructive diseases of the biliary tree (duct anomalies, cysts and tumours).

What are the common presenting features of chronic pancreatitis?

The common presenting features include continuous or intermittent severe abdominal pain with weight loss and jaundice. In the later stages, there is steatorrhoea and diabetes.

8.   ASBESTOS

What is the commonest form of asbestos?

The commonest form of asbestos is **chrysotile** which accounts for 95% of previous commercially used asbestos. It is otherwise known as **white asbestos**. The other forms of asbestos belong to the amphibole group, consisting of crocidolite (blue asbestos), amosite (brown asbestos), anthophyllite, tremolite and actinolyte.

What is the most important factor in determining the development of asbestosis?

The most important factor is the **amount of dust inhaled**. Heavy exposure for a few years or exposure to a fairly low concentration over many years are equally likely to result in asbestosis.

What happens to asbestos fibres once they are inhaled?

Inhaled asbestos fibres are retained mostly in the **respiratory bronchioles of the lower lobes**. The short fibres are readily phagocytosed by macrophages, but fibres over 30 µm long are incompletely ingested. Macrophages subsequently surround these asbestos fibres which become coated with an endogenous iron protein, to produce the characteristic **asbestos body**. The asbestos directly stimulates macrophages to secrete fibrogenic lysosomal enzymes.

What lung problems does asbestos cause?

Asbestos causes fibrosis. The disease commences in the sub-pleural region of the lower lobes and causes fibrous thickening of the visceral pleura. Fibrosis then progresses inwards and upwards so that the middle lobe and lower parts of the upper lobes may be affected. There is progressive obliteration of the alveolar spaces with compensatory dilatation of the unaffected bronchioles.

What conditions does asbestos predispose to?

Asbestosis predisposes to the development of bronchial adenocarcinoma (occurs in nearly 50% of cases). Exposure to asbestos dust may also lead to the development of mesothelioma of the pleura or peritoneum.

Which type of asbestos is most frequently associated with mesothelioma?

Blue asbestos (Crocidolite).

9.   AMYLOID

What is amyloid?

Amyloid is a relatively inert substance composed of a group of pathological extracellular, proteinaceous substances whose main constituent is protein fibrils. Amyloid causes its pathological effects by accumulating in body tissues, either locally or systemically.

What tests can be used to identify amyloid?

Amyloid stains an orange colour with **Congo red stain** and gives a characteristic **green birefringence** when viewed under polarised light. Alternatively, amyloid may be identified using electron microscopy and methyl violet. However, Congo red is the most reliable method for identifying amyloid.

Apart from biopsy of the involved part, where else might you obtain a tissue sample to help make a diagnosis of amyloidosis?

Rectal mucosa or gingiva. The gastrointestinal tract is frequently involved in most types of amyloidosis (90% systemic). In addition, should haemorrhage occur it can be easily controlled.

What are the different types of amyloidosis?

Amyloidosis may be classified into four groups

- **Primary amyloidosis**, where there is no preceding disease
- **Secondary amyloidosis**, which is a complication of a usually chronic disease condition, usually inflammatory (rheumatoid arthritis, Crohn's disease) or infectious (tuberculosis, leprosy)
- **Familial amyloidosis**
- **Isolated amyloidosis**, which is organ limited, such as the brain of Alzheimer's patients

What part of the body does amyloid disease affect?

GI tract, kidney, heart, liver, spleen, lung.

What clinical effects does it produce?

- **GI tract**   Common
                        Any part
                        May produce obstruction, haemorrhage, protein enteropathy, malabsorption, ulceration, diarrhoea
- **Kidney**   Common
                        Deposition in the glomeruli, arterioles and interstitial tissue (most common presenting feature).
                        May produce nephrotic syndrome, renal vein thrombosis, haematuria, proteinuria.

- **Cardiac**   Usually in elderly people
                   Cardiomegaly and heart failure
                   Dysrhythmias
- **Liver**   Causes atrophy
                   Rarely causes liver failure or portal
                   hypertension
- **Spleen**   Translucent nodules seen (Sago
                   spleen)
- **Respiratory** Multiple nodules and diffuse
                   involvement of the lung parenchyma
                   and tracheobronchial tree
                   Haemoptysis and respiratory failure

10.   GRAM STAINING

What is the principle of the Gram stain?

The Gram stain works on the principle that certain bacteria are able to retain an **iodine purple dye complex** when exposed to a brief alcohol wash. Gram-negative bacteria have a smaller cell wall but a higher lipid content and as a result, the alcohol washes away the purple dye. Gram-positive bacteria appear blue and Gram-negative bacteria are counter-stained with a pink dye.

What steps are involved in the Gram staining process?

The Gram staining process involves

- First, exposing the bacteria to a **crystal violet and iodine solution**
- Subsequently, an **alcohol wash** is performed. Gram-positive bacteria retain the purple complex and remain purple, whereas Gram-negative bacteria are pale.
- **Counter-staining** with safranine (pink dye) turns the Gram-negative bacteria pink so that they become visible

Can you name some common bacterial cocci that are Gram-positive and describe what clinical infections they produce?

Staphylococcus aureus is an example of a Gram-positive coccus. *S. aureus* is a commensal carried in the nose, pharynx and perineum of normal individuals. It produces skin infections such as pustules, carbuncles and boils. It is also implicated in wound infection and pneumonia (nosocomial or following an episode of influenza).

Streptococcus pyogenes is another common Gram-positive coccus and is responsible for skin infections such as impetigo, erysipelas, cellulitis and tonsillitis. It may also be a commensal of the pharynx in normal individuals.

Can you name some common bacteria that are Gram-negative and describe what clinical infections they produce?

Neisseria meningitidis is an example of a Gram-negative coccus. It is a known commensal of the nasopharynx. It may cause purulent meningitis and fatal septicaemia.

Neisseria gonorrhoea is another example of a Gram-negative coccus. It is responsible for genitourinary tract infections such as urethritis, prostatitis, epididymitis, salpingitis and perihepatitis. It may also give rise to a reactive arthritis affecting the large joints such as the knee. It is a known commensal of the genital mucosa.

Examples of Gram-negative bacilli include **aerobic coliforms** (*E.coli*, Proteus and Klebsiella) and the **anaerobic *Bacteroides fragilis***. These bacteria can give rise to infections of the alimentary and urinary tracts such as appendicitis, diverticulitis, pyelonephritis and cystitis. They are also gastrointestinal commensals.

What bacteria produce gas gangrene?

Gas gangrene is produced by bacteria of the **Clostridia group** (usually *Clostridia perfringens*) which infect wounds that are devascularised and have poor oxygen tension. The Clostridia group of bacteria are Gram-positive, anaerobic bacilli. They produce proteolytic enzymes which result in digestion of muscle tissue with gas formation.

What is Beta-Lactamase?

Beta-Lactamase is an enzyme produced by bacteria such as *Staphylococcus aureus*. This enzyme can neutralise antibiotics such as penicillins and some cephalosporins, as they contain a Beta-Lactam ring as part of their molecular structure.

What is the mechanism of action of the Beta-Lactam antibiotics?

The Beta-Lactam antibiotics (penicillin and cephalosporin) inhibit the production of Murein, the main constituent of the bacterial cell wall.

11.   BLOOD TRANSFUSION

What blood products are available for use in surgical patients?

Available blood products include

- Packed cells (storage life of 35–42 days)
- Platelet concentrates (shelf life of 5 days) there are no viable platelets in stored blood after 48 hours
- Granulocyte concentrates
- Fresh Frozen Plasma (plasma that has been separated from red cells within 6 hours of collection. It contains all the coagulation factors and can be stored for up to 1 year. When thawed it should be used immediately.)
- Cryoprecipitate (contains factor VIII, fibrinogen and von Willebrand factor)

What are the complications of blood transfusion?

Complications may be classified into **immune related** and **non-immune related**.

Immune related complications include

- **Minor**: fever following transfusion of donor pyrogens or allergy to degradation products of leucocytes
- **Major**: ABO and Rhesus incompatibility

The severity of the incompatibility reaction is dependent on the transfusion rate and the strength of the antibody. Donor blood cells (antigen) react with the recipient's antibodies to produce agglutination and haemolysis. The resultant haemolysis causing loin pain, haemoglobulinaemia and shock.

Non-immune complications are usually biochemical or volume related.

- **Hypocalcaemia** (common) occurs because the citrate used to preserve the blood during storage binds calcium
- **Hyperkalaemia** (common) occurs as there is often lysed red blood cells in the transfused packed cell units
- **Circulatory overload** can precipitate heart failure if the transfusion is too rapid or excessive.
- **Infections** with Hepatitis B and C, HIV, syphilis and malaria

What are the possible benefits of autologous transfusion?

Autologous transfusion may reduce the risks of incompatibility, transfusion reactions and exposure to possible transferable infections. It may also reduce the burden on the blood transfusion donor service.

Can you explain the genetics of the ABO blood groups?

Blood group antigens are inherited in a simple Mendelian manner. The alleles A and B are equally expressed or co-dominant, whereas the O allele has no observable expression. Therefore, the genotypes and phenotypes are as follows:

Genotype	Phenotype
AA	A
AO	A
AB	AB
BO	B
BB	B
OO	O

12. SURGICAL CONSENT

What are the main objectives in obtaining informed consent?

Informed consent pre-supposes a joint decision and agreement between the doctor and patient. It should now be considered a discussion between the doctor and patient, and include

- A description of the procedure, including a probable prognosis
- The likelihood of specific and general complications of the procedure
- Information about alternative options and risks incurred by doing nothing

Patients should participate and share in decisions and give active, not passive, comment.

Who can give valid written consent?

All competent patients over the age of 16 years may sign the consent form. The clinician obtaining consent must also countersign the form.

What are the principles of good consenting practice?

- A suitable environment should be used, i.e. private and free from possible interruptions
- Simple language which is understood by patients and their relatives
- Confirmation that the patient has understood the procedure, by asking him/her to re-explain the procedure and whether any questions remain unanswered.
- Find out patient's individual needs and priorities when providing information about treatment options.

What is the meaning of valid consent?

Valid consent is one that is given voluntarily by an appropriately informed person who has the capacity to consent to the intervention in question.

How should you obtain consent for children?

Consent should be obtained from a person – usually the parent or designated legal guardian – deemed competent to make informed choices about the child's best interests. In some circumstances consent may be obtained from a child below 16 years old if they are mature enough to understand the nature, purpose and possible consequences of the proposed treatment, as well as the consequences of non-treatment (i.e. *Gillick* competent). However, they should be encouraged to communicate with their parents/legal guardian.

What is the accepted practice for consenting an unconscious adult patient for an emergency operation?

It is the surgeon's responsibility to act in the patient's best interests. Therefore, surgery without consent is permitted if deemed life saving. Relatives cannot legally consent to surgery because no adult can legally consent on behalf of another.

What is the accepted practice for consenting a mentally ill or handicapped person for an emergency operation?

In the emergency situation, if the patient is believed to be incompetent and unable to understand and give informed consent, the surgeon should proceed with treatment in the patient's best interests.

13.   DIABETES IN SURGERY

Why are diabetic patients high-risk surgical candidates?

Diabetic patients are high-risk surgical candidates because they often have

- Co-existing cardiovascular disease (hypertension, angina, previous CVA and atherosclerosis)
- Increased risk of metabolic disturbance (hyperglycaemia and ketoacidosis)
- Co-existing renal disease
- Poor wound healing
- An increased probability of infection

How might these surgical risks be minimised?

These risks may be minimised by pre-operative correction of any cardiovascular and metabolic problems and optimisation of their current clinical status.

Throughout the peri-operative period the blood glucose level must be kept stable. This will decrease the risk of metabolic disturbance and reduce the probability of infection.

The precise method of controlling blood glucose levels depends on the severity of the diabetes and whether the surgery being undertaken is major or minor.

How are diabetic patients managed in the peri-operative period?

Diabetes can be classified as IDDM (insulin dependent diabetes mellitus) or NIDDM (non-insulin dependent diabetes mellitus).

IDDM: **Insulin controlled**
NIDDM: **Oral hypoglycaemic controlled**
              Diet controlled

- For **diet controlled patients** undergoing minor surgery no additional precautions to the normal daily routine of blood glucose monitoring need to be taken. However, when undergoing major surgery these patients require hourly blood glucose monitoring. An insulin sliding scale is started and the glucose is maintained between 7 and 10 mmol/l.

- For **oral hypoglycaemic controlled patients** who are undergoing minor surgery, the morning dose of oral hypoglycaemic agent should be omitted. Blood glucose is monitored 4 hourly and the oral hypoglycaemic drug is recommended only when the patient is eating and drinking normally. When these patients are undergoing major surgery, an insulin sliding scale is used to control the blood glucose. This regimen is commenced when the patient is starved for surgery and stopped when the patient is eating and drinking normally and has no electrolyte disturbance.

- For **insulin controlled patients** undergoing only very minor surgery the insulin dose is omitted whilst nil by mouth. Otherwise, these patients are managed with an insulin sliding scale and dextrose infusion until normal dietary fluid and intake are resumed.

Metformin omitted c̄ contrast.

14. POST-OPERATIVE ANALGESIA

What are the principles of post-operative pain management?

Management of post-operative pain should be tailored to the individual patient. It is important to choose the appropriate drug and mode of delivery. Provision of post-operative pain relief can be divided into pre-operative, intra-operative and post-operative methods.

- **Pre-operative**

This includes pre-emptive analgesia with NSAIDs or nerve blocks. Epidural analgesia given 48 hrs before lower limb amputation has been shown to reduce the incidence of phantom limb pain. Pain is a subjective phenomenon and patient counselling is important (has been demonstrated to reduce post-operative pain).

- **Intra-operative**

Judicious use of opioids, regional nerve (including central and peripheral nerve) blocks and wound infiltration with local anaesthetic agents.

- **Post-operative**

Pain can be managed by either opioid or non-opioid methods.

Can you expand on the methods of post-operative pain relief?

Post-operative analgesia should be delivered according to an **analgesia ladder**, starting with the least potent agent and working upwards.

It is important to maintain adequate levels of analgesia rather than to provide analgesia solely on demand. A multi-modal approach is thought to be superior to single modal techniques.

Methods of providing post-operative pain relief may be broadly divided into

- Drug therapy
- Regional anaesthetic techniques
- Psychological methods

Drug therapy would encompass opioid and non-opioid methods. The opioid drugs, for example, include morphine, diamorphine and pethidine. The non-opioid drugs include most commonly NSAIDs and paracetamol (+/- combinations).

Regional anaesthetic techniques include central, neuraxial blocks e.g. epidural (usually a combination of opioid and local anaesthetic), spinal nerve blocks (fentanyl or diamorphine and bupivacaine) and peripheral nerve blocks (intercostal, brachial or local infiltration).

Psychological methods are important and include psycho-prophylaxis and relaxation techniques.

When considering these methods one needs to take into account the route of administration – parenteral (intra-muscular, intravenous, continuous infusion, patient controlled analgesia (PCA)) and non-parenteral (oral, buccal, sublingual, rectal, transdermal, intra-articular, spinal, TENS (trans-cutaneous electrical nerve stimulation) and inhalational).

What are the advantages of patient controlled analgesia (PCA)?

PCA provides rapid prompt drug delivery. Studies have shown that it gives greater patient satisfaction and improves ventilation compared with conventional routes of analgesia administration.

What are the physiological benefits of good post-operative pain control?

Pain produces a stressor effect on the body. Thus, effective analgesia will reduce this response and therefore benefit the respiratory, cardiovascular, gastrointestinal and genitourinary systems.

With good pain relief there is

- Improved respiratory function as a result of reduced splinting of the diaphragm and subsequent increased alveolar ventilation. This further reduces the risk of hypoxia.
- Reduced sympathetic stimulation, so decreasing cardiac work and systemic vascular resistance. This in turn improves splanchnic and renal perfusion.
- Reduced incidence of deep venous thrombosis, due to more rapid patient mobilisation
- Reduced incidence of post-operative ileus and urinary retention

15.   SCREENING AND SURGERY

What are the important components of a good screening test?

A good screening test should be sensitive and specific. It must be safe, relatively inexpensive and capable of achieving adequate compliance in the population to be screened.

What do you understand by the sensitivity of a screening test?

The sensitivity of a screening test refers to the ability to detect the cases with the specified condition with few false-negative results i.e. "the proportion of diseased patients who are reported as positive."

$$\text{Sensitivity} = \frac{\text{True positives}}{\text{Total number of final diagnosis positive}}$$

What is meant by specificity of a screening test?

Specificity of a screening test refers to the degree to which only the specified condition is detected with few false positive results i.e. "proportion of disease-free patients who are reported as negative."

$$\text{Specificity} = \frac{\text{True negative}}{\text{Total number of final diagnosis negative}}$$

What is the minimum accepted compliance rate for a screening test to be successful?

In practice, one would like to achieve at least a 70% compliance rate within the screened population.

What screening tests have been shown to reduce the mortality from colorectal cancer?

There are two screening tests that have been shown to reduce mortality: **faecal occult blood** (FOB) testing and **sigmoidoscopy**. Two randomised controlled trials (Nottingham and Denmark) have demonstrated that biennial FOB testing reduces the risk of colorectal cancer by between 15–18% in the normal population. Another trial in the United States has demonstrated a reduction in mortality of 33% with annual testing. Retrospective case control studies have demonstrated a 60% reduction in mortality of cancers within the reach of the rigid sigmoidoscope.

At present, there are two ongoing trials evaluating colorectal cancer screening. The first is a prospective control trial of once-only flexible sigmoidoscopy between the ages of 55 and 64 years (MRC/NHS flexible sigmoidoscopy). The second is a FOB screening programme which is being performed in two pilot centres.

Who do you think should be screened for colorectal cancer in the UK?

This is a matter of debate, but high-risk individuals (namely those who have a first degree relative who developed colorectal cancer before the age of 45 years (lifetime risk 1:10) or worse), or those with a family history of familial adenomatous polyposis (FAP) or hereditary non-polyposis colon cancer (HNPCC).

Another group which one commonly encounters is 'normal' risk individuals who are anxious about colorectal cancer. They should be informed of the limitations and the risks of the screening. Having discussed the risks/benefits these individuals may be offered a faecal occult blood test and if found to be positive, progress to colonoscopy.

16.   STOMA

What are the uses of a stoma?
Stomas can be used for drainage, enteral feeding or faecal stream diversion.

Can you elaborate on this?
Stomas may be classified into **temporary** or **permanent**.

Temporary stomas include

- **Input stomas into the stomach or jejunum** to allow feeding into the upper gastrointestinal tract, avoiding the need for a nasogastric tube.
- A **pharyngostomy** or **oesophagostomy**, which are used to divert solids and saliva to protect the bronchial tree in neonates with oesophageal atresia or tracheo-oesophageal fistula.
- **Caecostomy**, which is occasionally used for decompression of the large bowel (more frequently in the USA)

Another use of a temporary stoma is to divert faecal material away from a diseased part of the bowel or to allow healing of a distal anastomosis. This includes a **loop ileostomy** or **colostomy**, for example following a low anterior resection.

Examples of a **permanent stoma** include an **end colostomy** following an abdomino-perineal resection or an **end ileostomy** following a pan-proctocolectomy.

What are the principles of siting a stoma?
Ideally, a stoma should be sited pre-operatively in the most favourable position for the patient, away from bony prominences. The stoma must be in a position which would be easy for the patient to manage and change.

How do you differentiate clinically between a colostomy and ileostomy?
An end colostomy is normally located in the left iliac fossa. A transverse loop colostomy is usually situated in the upper quadrants of the abdomen. A colostomy can be differentiated from an ileostomy in that the bowel mucosa is usually flush with the skin. An ileostomy has a spout which is fashioned to prevent excoriation of the skin by the succus entericus.

What stoma complications do you know of?
Stoma complications may be divided into immediate, early and late.

- **Immediate complications** include bleeding and ischaemia (early ischaemia is usually the result of technical failure).
- **Early complications** include high output which is not uncommon in patients who have loop or end ileostomies. High output is common in the post-operative period and

the patient may lose a considerable volume of fluid. Other complications include obstruction and retraction.
* **Late complications** include obstruction, poor siting, prolapse, parastomal hernia, skin excoriation, skin hypersensitivity, fistula formation and psychological morbidity.

17.   MALIGNANT MELANOMA

What are the risk factors for malignant melanoma?

- Fair skin
- Albinism
- Previous melanoma
- Intermittent sunlight exposure (ultraviolet light - continuous exposure causes basal cell and squamous cell carcinomas)
- Family history of dysplastic naevi
- Xeroderma pigmentosa
- Family history

What are Clarke's levels and Breslow's thickness?

Breslow describes the thickness of the tumour in millimetres, whereas Clarke describes a level of invasion (epidermis, dermis, subcutaneous fat). Breslow's thickness has been shown to be a superior indicator of prognosis, as Clarke's levels are based on the thickness of the reticular dermis which varies considerably around the body.

Can you name any other prognostic indicators?

Factors associated with poor prognosis include

- Increasing age (high mitotic rate on histology)
- Ulceration
- Male gender
- Site (in order of poorer prognosis: lower limb, upper limb, trunk, head and neck)

What is the mainstay treatment of melanoma?

Excision of the melanoma forms the mainstay treatment. The most effective and safe margins of excision are currently being evaluated. For melanoma <0.76 mm thick, the width of surgical excision does not appear to be important in the overall outcome. 1 cm margins have been shown to be effective for treatment of melanomas ≤ 2 mm thick.

What is the role of adjuvant therapy in the treatment of melanoma?

At present, no single or combination chemotherapy regimens have been shown to improve mortality in malignant melanoma. Melanoma is also very radio-resistant. Isolated limb perfusion is performed in a few centres for the control of in-transit, poor prognosis and satellite lesions, however with variable results. Its precise role in adjuvant therapy has not been established and should only be undertaken in the setting of a prospective randomised controlled trial.

18.   HIV INFECTION

What are the high risk groups for HIV infection?

Homosexual males; IV drug abusers; haemophiliacs before 1985; children of infected mothers; patients from endemic areas (Africa, SE Asia).

However, the latest figures from the Public Health laboratory show that the incidence of HIV infection is higher in heterosexual than in homosexual males.

What cancers are particularly associated with HIV infection?

Cervical carcinoma, anal carcinoma, Kaposi's sarcoma, high grade lymphoma (Non-Hodgkin's Lymphoma).

How is HIV infection commonly transmitted in healthcare workers?

Needle stick injury, mucosal contact or contamination of a non-intact skin surface.

What is the risk of HIV infection after accidental exposure to infected blood or body fluids?

The average risk of HIV infection after a single percutaneous exposure is 0.3%. The risk is lower if there is contamination of non-intact skin, but higher if there is conjunctival contamination with blood.

What factors increase the risk of sero-conversion following needle-stick injury?

The factors include exposure to a large inoculum of infected blood, (as indicated by a deep injury, visible blood on the device) procedures entailing needles placed directly into blood vessels and a source patient with terminal HIV infection.

What are the guidelines regarding post-exposure prophylaxis?

In the UK, prophylaxis is recommended for exposed workers who are at high risk of infection (see answer to previous question above). In addition, risk assessment should include details of the exposure, CD4 count, viral load and anti-retroviral history of the source patient.

Counselling forms an important part of the management and the exposed health worker needs to be fully informed of the risks, the rationale for treatment. The relative lack of data means that the final decision rests in the health worker's hands.

Presently, triple therapy is given in the form of Zidovudine, Lamivudine and the protease inhibitor Indinavir for six months. This regimen is commenced as soon as possible.

What is the rationale for giving prophylactic medication?

The rationale is that the uptake of HIV and processing of its antigen may take several hours or days. Thus, there is a window for therapeutic intervention following accidental inoculation. In addition, anti-retroviral therapy may modify the clinical course of the disease.

19.   URINARY TRACT CALCULI

What are the main types of urinary calculi?

The main types of urinary tract calculi are

- **Calcium oxalate +/- calcium phosphate** (most common type 70%)
- **Uric acid** (mixture of uric acids and urates – 5%)
- Complex **triple phosphate** stones. Magnesium ammonia phosphate (often in conjunction with calcium phosphate) 15–20%.
- **Cysteine** stones (2%)

What are predisposing factors for calcium stone formation?

The risk factors include conditions causing hypercalciuria, hyperoxaluria, ↑ pH and low volume of urine. These lead to supersaturation of calcium oxalate and calcium phosphate.

Thus, conditions such as urinary tract obstruction, infection, prolonged bedrest, renal tubular acidosis, medullary sponge kidney, hyperparathyroidism and excess vitamin D all predispose to calcium containing stones.

Stones may also form when various substances act as a nidus for stone formation e.g. foreign body, non-absorbable sutures, carcinoma, necrotic papillae.

Which urinary tract calculi are radiolucent?

Uric acid, xanthine and matrix (mucoprotein) stones are radiolucent.

Are men or women more likely to develop urinary calculi?

Men are three times more likely to develop stones than women.

What is the most common age of presentation?

Between 30 and 50 years.

What symptoms does a stone in the ureter cause?

Symptoms include segmental referred pain to the groin or testicle, loin pain, haematuria, frequency, vomiting, constipation and diarrhoea.

What proportion of ureteral calculi pass spontaneously?

50%.

20.   INTESTINAL FISTULAE

What is the definition of a fistula?

A fistula is an abnormal communication between two epithelial lined surfaces lined by chronic granulation tissue.

How do you classify gastrointestinal fistulae?

Fistulae may be **congenital or acquired**.

An example of a congenital fistula is a tracheo-oesophageal fistula.

Acquired fistulae may be subdivided into **inflammatory, neoplastic, traumatic and infective**. Inflammatory fistulae include those secondary to Crohn's disease, diverticular disease or pancreatitis. Neoplastic fistulae usually arise from colon cancer. Traumatic fistulae may occur secondary to surgery, radiation or any penetrating injury. Infective causes include conditions such as actinomycosis and tuberculosis.

Do you know of another way of classifying fistulae?

Fistulae may be classified according to their output in a 24 hr period (low output <200 ml per 24 hr period, moderate output 200–500 ml per 24 hr period and high output >500 ml per 24 hr period) or anatomical location in the gastrointestinal tract.

Why is the output of a fistula important?

Precise knowledge of fistula output is essential because it is an independent predictor of spontaneous closure. Patients with high output fistulae (in practice those of >1500 ml/24 hr) usually have a poorer prognosis because of greater loss of fluid, electrolytes, minerals, trace elements and protein.

What is the role of radiological investigations in the management of an entero-cutaneous fistula?

The main role of investigation is to provide information about the **anatomical localisation** of the fistula. Helpful investigations include plain radiography, GI contrast studies, fistulograms, ultrasound and CT.

Can you outline the overall principles of management of an enterocutaneous fistula?

The management may be divided into three phases

- **Diagnosis and recognition**
- **Stabilisation and investigation**
- **Definitive care**

The goal in the stabilisation phase is to **control complications** such as fluid and electrolyte abnormalities, sepsis and malnutrition if present. This involves **resuscitation of the patient** and consideration for transfer to a surgical high-dependency unit or ICU for monitoring, and/or organ support, if deemed appropriate. Correction of fluid, electrolyte and nutritional imbalances should be performed as soon as possible.

Drainage of sepsis or abscesses should be performed, the skin protected from corrosive enteric enzymes and bile salts, **placement of a nasogastric tube**, initiation of a **proton pump inhibitor** and **total parenteral nutrition** (if the fistula renders most of the gastrointestinal tract unavailable for enteric feeding) should be considered.

What features would be unfavourable for spontaneous closure of an enterocutaneous fistula?

Unfavourable features would include the presence of an adjacent abscess or diseased bowel, intestinal disruption, distal obstruction, presence of a foreign body, irradiated bowel, epithelisation of a fistulous tract or presence of a neoplasm.

Locations that are particularly unfavourable to spontaneous closure include the stomach, duodenum and ileum. As a general rule, if a fistula has not closed by six weeks of medical management, it is unlikely to close without surgical intervention.

What operative interventions might be appropriate in the management of an enterocutaneous fistula?

Appropriate operative interventions would include resection of the diseased segment with primary anastomosis. If the fistula opening cannot be closed or resected, exteriorisation or serosal patch using jejunum or defunctioning Roux loop are other possible options. It is important to say that the operation should address the underlying cause of the fistula formation if possible.

21.   ALCOHOL

What are the adverse effects of alcohol?

Alcohol adversely affects numerous systems within the body.

- **Nervous system** – psychological disturbances leading to depression, anxiety, memory disturbances (including Wernicke-Korsakoff syndrome), cerebral atrophy, cerebellar degeneration, thiamine deficiencies and polyneuropathy.
- **Cardiac** – dilated cardiomyopathy
- **Liver** – alcoholic liver disease (fatty change hepatitis, cirrhosis)
- **Pancreas** – pancreatitis
- **Stomach** and Duodenum – ulceration

↓ Haematopoietic system → ↓ Clotting. Immune system probs.

What effects does alcohol have on the liver?

Alcohol can lead to a wide spectrum of liver problems, including **fatty change, hepatitis and cirrhosis**. Fatty change is due to malnutrition and the direct metabolic insults.

What histological changes are seen in the liver?

In alcoholic hepatitis, there is cellular necrosis and infiltration with polymorphonuclear leucocytes. The hepatocytes occasionally contain eosinophilic structures called Mallory bodies, which consist of a meshwork of fibrils in an area where the rough endoplasmic reticulum has broken up. In alcoholic cirrhosis, there is destruction and fibrosis seen in regenerating nodules. In addition, there is also bridging fibrosis between the portal tracts and terminal hepatic veins.

Are Mallory bodies pathogno-monic of alcoholic cirrhosis?

No, Mallory bodies are suggestive of alcoholic liver damage but they are seen in other conditions such as primary biliary cirrhosis.

What types of anaemia are associated with chronic alcohol ingestion?

The most common anaemia seen with alcohol abuse is a **megaloblastic anaemia**. This is usually due to a folate deficiency. Folate deficiency is usually due to inadequate dietary intake, but may also be due to disorders of metabolism by the liver. Occasionally anaemia of chronic disease and **sideroblastic anaemia** may be seen. (Sideroblastic anaemia is a condition of hypochromic anaemia with the presence of abnormal sideroblasts in the marrow.)

What happens to vitamin B_{12} levels in alcoholic cirrhosis?

Vitamin B_{12} levels remain normal or are increased.

What types of cancer are associated with alcohol?

There is evidence that alcohol interacts with tobacco smoke and other agents to cause cancer of the **mouth**, **pharynx**, **larynx** and **oesophagus**. Pure alcohol *per se* is not carcinogenic, but alcohol may render other agents soluble or it may be that the carcinogenic agent is another component of alcoholic drinks. Cancer of the **liver** is the other major tumour associated, over 80% of hepatocellular carcinomas arise in cirrhotic livers.

22.   INFANTILE HYPERTROPHIC PYLORIC STENOSIS

How common is infantile hypertrophic pyloric stenosis?

3:1000 births and characteristically first-born male infants are most commonly affected.

When do symptoms occur?

Usually between the 3rd and 6th weeks of life.

What are the classic features?

Forcible, projectile vomiting (no bile) is the presenting feature in all cases. Visible peristalsis, a palpable lump beneath the liver, constipation and loss of weight

What metabolic effects are associated with infantile hypertrophic pyloric stenosis?

The main metabolic effect of pyloric stenosis is related to dehydration following vomiting. Classically, it causes a hypokalaemic, hypochloraemic metabolic alkalosis. Mild uraemia and haemoconcentration may occur due to volume depletion.

What effect does metabolic alkalosis have on respiration?

In metabolic alkalosis, the increase in extracellular pH reduces the stimulus for ventilation via the brain stem chemoreceptors. This produces depression of the respiratory centre and results in slow shallow respirations.

What effect does pyloric stenosis have on the oxygen dissociation curve?

Pyloric stenosis increases the extracellular pH and therefore shifts the oxygen curve to the left. This interferes with oxygen release to tissues.

Can you name any other causes of metabolic alkalosis?

The other common causes of metabolic alkalosis are due to excessive intake of bicarbonates such as ingestion of antacids, or excessive loss of hydrogen ions, for example following nasogastric aspiration, diuretic therapy, Cushing's syndrome or primary hyperaldosteronism.

How would you treat hyper-trophic pyloric stenosis?

After correcting fluid and electrolyte abnormalities, the child may undergo a Ramstedt's pyloromyotomy.

Can you describe what is done in a Ramstedt's operation?

The hypertrophic muscle is split transversely from the stomach to the duodenum. The two halves are spread widely at the submucosal plaque and the lumen is not entered.

Are there any long-term problems?

No, prognosis is excellent and complications are relatively uncommon.

23.   LEG ULCERS

What are the common causes of leg ulcers?

Ulceration may occur in the lower limb as a result of **venous disease**, **diabetes mellitus**, peripheral **neuropathy**, **peripheral atherosclerosis**, **rheumatoid disease**, **trauma**, **malignancy** (basal cell carcinoma, squamous cell carcinoma and malignant melanoma) and **vasculitic disorders** such as systemic lupus erythematosus.

What is the most common cause of leg ulceration in the UK?

The most common cause of leg ulceration in the UK is **venous ulceration**.

What is your initial management of a patient presenting with a venous looking ulcer?

I would take a **full history and examination** in the first instance to ascertain the aetiology of this ulceration. Clinical examination is important as the position, size, shape and location of the ulcer will usually give a good indication as to the underlying pathology. The presence of lipodermatosclerosis and/or varicose veins strongly suggests a venous aetiology. If a venous ulcer is suspected, **duplex ultrasonography** must be carried out.

How are venous ulcers treated?

The mainstay treatment is compression bandaging using a 3 or 4 layer technique. Compression stockings may also be used and class 2 or 3 compression hosiery is most appropriate for patients with venous ulceration.

Does surgery have a place in the treatment of patients with venous ulceration?

Yes. Surgical treatment of superficial venous incompetence and varicose veins (identified with duplex Doppler ultrasound) could result in ulcer healing if deemed the cause of venous ulceration. In resistant cases, split skin grafting of ulcers may be used.

24.   LUNG CARCINOMA

What are the common presenting symptoms of a lung carcinoma?

A patient with lung carcinoma may present with symptoms of the **primary tumour, secondary spread, paraneoplastic syndromes** (rare) or **generalised features of malignancy**.

The common **primary tumour symptoms** are cough, pleuritic chest pain, haemoptosis, shortness of breath, hoarseness and recurrent chest infections.

not a symptom

Symptoms of secondary spread include bone pain, hepato-megaly, focal neurological signs with changes in personality or epilepsy due to metastatic deposits in the brain.

The **common generalised symptoms** are weight loss and anorexia.

Lung carcinoma may occasionally present with **paraneoplastic syndromes** including hypertrophic pulmonary osteoarthropathy, syndrome of inappropriate ADH secretion (SIADH), ectopic ACTH or neurological symptoms including Eaton-Lambert syndrome (polymyopathy and myasthenic syndrome).

How might you assess the suitability of a patient with known lung cancer for surgical treatment?

Two principles are involved in the assessment for surgical treatment. Firstly, an adequate level of patient fitness to tolerate an extensive pulmonary resection and secondly, a tumour that is sufficiently localised to permit complete resection.

The assessment first starts clinically, one needs to closely examine the medical history, exercise tolerance and take into account the age of the patient.

The investigations would include lung function tests which would give a general guide to see whether pneumonectomy is feasible. An FEV_1 exceeding 1.5 litres and an FEV_1/FVC ratio >50% would indicate that a pneumonectomy would be possible.

The tumour would also require staging – intra-thoracic staging is carried out using chest X-ray and CT. Mediastinoscopy may be used to evaluate the supra-mediastinal lymph nodes and help determine resectability. More recently, video assisted thoraco-scopic surgery has been used to assess involvement of mediastinal nodes which are enlarged on CT and lie beyond the reach of mediastinoscopy.

Extra-thoracic staging involves searching for distant metastases, which may be evident from history and examination.

Further evaluation would include a bone scan, ultrasound of liver, CT of brain and abdomen, looking particularly at the liver and adrenal glands. Positron emission tomography (PET) has been used to detect metastatic deposits and may help characterise abnormalities seen on CT scan.

What are the four main histological types of lung cancer?

The four types of lung cancer are the small cell carcinoma (25%), squamous cell carcinoma (35%), adenocarcinoma (25%) and large cell undifferentiated carcinoma (14%).

Which one of these is amenable for surgical resection?

Less then 5% of small cell carcinomas are suitable for surgical resection. In the majority of instances chemotherapy is the treatment of choice but survival is usually only months. For non-small cell carcinoma surgical resection is possible in approximately 10–15% of cases. In the majority of cases the disease is advanced and this precludes surgical intervention. Chemotherapy is gaining importance in the treatment of non-small cell carcinoma.

25.   TRANSURETHRAL (TUR) SYNDROME

What is the transurethral (TUR) syndrome?

The transurethral (TUR) syndrome is a syndrome caused by a combination of fluid overload, hyponatraemia and in extreme cases haemolysis, as a result of the bladder irrigation fluid.

What factors increase the risk of development of TUR syndrome?

The use of hypotonic solutions or water and high pressures in the bladder are likely to increase the risk.

How does the TUR syndrome present?

TUR syndrome should be suspected if the patient becomes hypotensive or hypertensive during or shortly after the operation. There is often altered consciousness and mental impairment. This is usually due to the profound dilutional hyponatraemia and impaired respiratory function, caused by the fluid overload. Other features include nausea, vomiting, headache, fatigue, weakness, muscle twitching, seizures or coma. The urinary sodium is >20 mmol/l.

What are the other causes of hyponatraemia?

Hyponatraemia may be due to extracellular fluid volume depletion or extracellular fluid volume excess.

Causes of ECF volume depletion include

*   Osmotic diuresis
*   Diuretic excess
*   Mineralocorticoid deficiency

Causes of ECF volume excess include

*   Causes of inappropriate ADH secretion, such as neoplastic lesions (in the lung, pancreas or CNS lesions)
*   Glucocorticoid or thyroid deficiency
*   Hypothyroidism
*   Drugs such as carbamazepine
*   Acute on-chronic renal failure
*   Nephrotic syndrome
*   Cirrhosis
*   Heart failure

26. COLORECTAL CANCER

How many deaths does colorectal cancer cause in a year in the UK?

19,000 deaths.

What is the distribution of tumours in the colon and rectum?

When considering the entire large bowel

- Rectal cancer   37%
- Sigmoid carcinoma   27%
- Caecal carcinoma   14%
- Ascending colon cancer   7%
- Descending colon cancer   5%
- Transverse colonic cancer   4%
- Hepatic flexure   3%
- Splenic flexure   3%

How does colon cancer spread?

Colon cancer may spread directly, via the lymphatics, the blood or trans-coelomically. Lymphatic spread is the predominant mode of metastasis and tumour spreads from the paracolic nodes along the main colic arteries to reach the para-aortic glands in advanced disease. The most common site of blood-borne spread is the liver.

What staging systems are described for colorectal cancer?

Duke's staging is the most widely accepted clinical pathological staging method for colorectal cancer and is based on histological examination of the resected specimen (the original classification was used for rectal carcinoma). **Duke's A** is a carcinoma that does not breach the muscularis propria, **Duke's B** is a carcinoma that breaches the muscularis propria, but does not involve the regional lymph nodes. **Duke's C1** carcinoma involves the regional lymph nodes (apical node negative), **Duke's C2** carcinoma involves the regional lymph nodes (apical node positive). A later addition to the original Duke's staging was **Duke's stage D** which was based on clinical rather than pathological evidence and has come to represent the presence of distant metastases.

Other modifications have been described including the **Astler-Coller** and **TNM systems**. More recently, the United Kingdom Coordinating Committee for Cancer Research (UKCCCR) has described and standardised the clinicopathological assessment of colorectal cancer (1997). From this assessment one is able to categorise whether a patient has undergone a procedure that is curative, non-curative or indeterminate for cure.

What are the 5 year survival rates after operation for colonic cancer?	Duke's A 90%, Duke's B 65%, Duke's C 23%, Duke's D 5%.
What conditions predispose to the development of colon cancer?	Long-standing inflammatory bowel disease including ulcerative colitis and Crohn's disease, ureterosigmoidostomy and previous gastric surgery all predispose to development of colon cancer. Hereditary conditions such as Familial Adenomatous Polyposis, Hereditary Non-Polyposis Colorectal Cancer, Gardner's syndrome, Turcot's syndrome and Canada-Cronkhite syndrome all predispose to colorectal cancer.
What is the risk of dysplasia or malignancy change in ulcerative colitis?	The risk of dysplasia increases with the length of history being approximately 7% at 10 years and rising to 17% at 30 years. Total colitis patients have a much higher risk than those with only left-sided disease (19-fold versus 4-fold) increase compared to the normal population. c PSC risk ↑↑
Can you suggest an appropriate surveillance protocol for patients with pan-ulcerative colitis?	Biennial colonoscopy with serial biopsy to detect dysplasia after 8 years of total colitis.
What proportion of patients with colorectal cancer have metastatic deposits in the liver at time of presentation?	30%.
What is the role of surgery for hepatic metastases?	The most widely accepted criterion for resection is one to three resectable metastases in one lobe of the liver. However, one should not be dogmatic as many surgeons are performing more extensive resections as long as clear tumour resection margins can be achieved and at least 60% normal functioning liver is left behind. Careful selection is required in all cases. Hepatic resection with clear margins in the absence of extrahepatic metastasis has a 5-year survival rate of 25%.
What are the risk factors for local recurrence of colorectal cancer?	The risk factors include **tumour penetration** of the bowel wall and **lymph node involvement**.

Special factors relating to the tumour itself include **high histological grade lesions**, **diminished lymphatic reaction, neurovascular invasion**. All are associated with a poorer outcome.

Some surgical factors have been recognised as being associated with poor outcome and include **perforation**, bowel **obstruction** and **direct invasion** of adjacent organs. |

27.   NIPPLE DISCHARGE

What are the common causes of a nipple discharge?

Nipple discharge may be **physiological** or **pathological**.

A **physiological discharge** can be expressed manually in most parous women.

The **pathological causes** of nipple discharge include carcinoma (which is the most important) but only counts for about 10% of all cases. Other causes include intra-ductal papilloma, duct ectasia, periductal mastitis and galactorrhoea.

How might you tell if the duct discharge contains blood?

This can be tested easily using a haemoccult test card or haemostix.

Do you investigate all patients presenting with a nipple discharge?

No, patients with a nipple discharge that warrant further investigation are those with a bloody discharge, a troublesome persistent unilateral discharge, those over 60 years old, ifassociated with a lump or with any asymmetrical thickening.

What are the indications for surgery in a patient with a nipple discharge?

There are **few indications** for surgery in a patient presenting solely with nipple discharge and no other significant abnormality on examination. However, one may consider surgery if

- There is a persistent bloody discharge arising from a single duct
- There is a suspicious lesion on mammography or ultrasound scan
- The discharge is persistent, troublesome and copious and arising from a number of ducts

What surgical procedures are available for single duct discharge?

The procedure of choice for this is a microdochectomy.

Does microdochectomy affect subsequent breast feeding?

In the vast majority of cases difficulty in breast feeding following microdochectomy is uncommon. However, it is a recognised complication. In contrast, breast-feeding would not be possible following total duct excision, which is used for recurrent periductal mastitis or multi-ductal discharge.

28.   ULCERATIVE COLITIS

How common is ulcerative colitis (UC)?

The incidence of UC is approximately 1:10,000 population in the UK.

Is there any familial tendency?

Yes, there is evidence of increased risk in families of affected individuals. The risk is between 10–20% for individuals who have a first degree relative with UC.

What is the relationship between smoking and UC?

Smoking is protective against UC. Stopping smoking increases the risk of developing the disease and causes exacerbations in those patients in remission.

How would you define an acute severe attack of UC?

Acute severe attack may be defined clinically by the presence of

- Six or more bloody diarrhoeal stools per day
- Pyrexia
- Tachycardia
- Anaemia
- Weight loss
- Abdominal pain/tenderness

What blood tests would you request to assess the activity of UC?

- Haemoglobin
- Platelet count
- ESR
- C-reactive protein
- Serum albumin

What other tests can be used to assess extent and activity of UC?

- Plain abdominal X-ray looking for colonic dilatation and thumb printing
- Erect chest X-ray or lateral decubitus abdominal film if you suspect perforation
- Radio-labelled white cell scan (99Tc-HMPAO)
- Rigid or flexible sigmoidoscopy without excessive air insufflation

What is the initial supportive treatment for acute active UC?

- Intravenous fluid replacement ± blood transfusion
- Nutritional support (enteral or parenteral depending on the clinical state)
- DVT prophylaxis (UC patients are at high risk of developing thromboembolism)
- Avoidance of drugs such as NSAIDs, anti-diarrhoeals (loperamide, codeine phosphate), opioid analgesic, anti-spasmodics and anti-cholinergic agents as they may provoke colonic dilatation.

What is the specific medical treatment of acute severe UC?

Intravenous <u>corticosteroids</u> form the cornerstone of treatment. Hydrocortisone or methylprednisolone may be used. Cyclosporin and heparin are still undergoing evaluation. Oral azathioprine and 6 mercaptopurine work too slowly to be effective in the acute episodes.

What are the indications for surgery in UC?

In the **emergency situation**

- Perforation
- Bleeding
- Toxic dilatation
- Failure of aggressive medical treatment

In the **elective situation**

- Malignant transformation
- Steroid dependence
- Recurrent acute exacerbations
- Growth retardation in children

29.   VARICOSE VEINS

What tests would you carry out on a patient presenting with varicose veins?

I would first take a history, and clinical examination looking for the presence of skin changes, ulceration, distribution of veins and the type of the veins involved.

With regard to the actual tests, a tourniquet (Trendelenburg's test) may give additional information about the location of venous incompetence.

A superior method of assessing the competence of the superficial veins is to use continuous wave or hand-held Doppler ultrasound. This should be the minimum required investigation before considering any operation. Other tests which may be useful include colour duplex ultrasound and venography.

How reliable are these tests you mentioned?

The **tourniquet test** is somewhat unreliable even in experienced hands and does not give much information regarding the function of the veins.

Continuous wave or hand-held Doppler ultrasound allows the competence of the long and short saphenous veins to be assessed with some confidence but does not provide accurate anatomical data regarding the location of the venous abnormalities.

Colour duplex ultrasound is an excellent and valuable technique for providing accurate anatomical and functional information and is the investigation of choice in complicated/ complex cases.

Venography is an alternative to colour duplex ultrasound and provides excellent anatomical detail but suffers from the fact it is an invasive procedure, is quite painful and functional information is a little limited.

What are the principles of primary varicose vein surgery?

The principles of varicose vein surgery are to ligate any incompetent junction(s) or communication(s) with the deep veins. These most commonly occur at the sapheno-femoral junctions, sapheno-popliteal junction and the perforating veins. The second principle is to remove the associated saphenous trunk and all visible varicosities.

Do patients normally have more than one source of venous reflux?

No, patients most frequently have only one major source of venous incompetence and only in about 10% of patients are there two or more sources of venous reflux. The most common sites of reflux are the sapheno-femoral and sapheno-popliteal junctions.

What is the rationale for stripping the long saphenous vein?

The rationale is that if the sapheno-femoral junction is ligated without stripping the long saphenous vein, the long saphenous vein remains potentially patent and incompetent and may fill from its tributaries. This has been shown to result in a higher rate of recurrence.

Are there any problems associated with stripping the long saphenous vein?

There is an increased incidence of bruising and risk of cutaneous nerve injury if the vein is stripped. However, the risk of injury can be reduced by stripping the long saphenous vein to the thigh or upper calf. Techniques have been described to minimise the risk of nerve injury, such as the inverting stripping method or using a pin-stripper.

Why do recurrent varicose veins occur?

The most frequent cause of recurrence of varicose veins following surgery, is failure to ligate the saphenous vein at the sapheno-femoral junction. Failure to ligate and strip the saphenous vein leads to potential development of further varices arising from this junction. In some patients neo-vascularisation may account for recurrent varicose veins.

30.   HYPERTENSION

How would you classify hypertension?

I would classify hypertension into primary (or essential) and secondary causes.

How common is secondary hypertension?

Secondary hypertension is very much less common than essential hypertension and accounts for about 5% of all cases.

What are the causes of secondary hypertension?

The causes can be broadly divided into

- **Renal**   Renovascular diseases, chronic renal failure
- **Adrenal**   Conn's syndrome, Cushing's syndrome, Phaeochromocytoma
- **Endocrine**   Acromegaly, Thyrotoxicosis, Hypothyroidism
- **Miscellaneous**   Hyperparathyroidism, Pre-eclampsia, Renin-secreting tumours

What is the commonest renovascular condition that causes hypertension?

Renal artery stenosis.

What is the nature of this stenosis?

The stenosis is usually due to fibromuscular dysplasia or atheroma.

What is the mechanism of this hypertension?

According to Goldblatt, constriction of the renal artery leads to a transient rise in renin levels, lasting up to a few weeks. After this period, renin levels return to normal. However, continued hypertension is seen. The precise mechanism is unknown but may involve another renal pressor agent or decreased secretion of another renal vasodilator substance. An alternative hypothesis is that patients become abnormally sensitive to angiotensin II.

How does Conn's syndrome cause hypertension?

In Conn's syndrome, there are raised levels of the mineralo-corticoid, aldosterone. Aldosterone stimulates sodium and water retention, so leading to elevated blood pressure.

What is the cause of Conn's syndrome?

In 80% cases it is due to an adrenal adenoma. In rare instances it is due to a carcinoma, and occasionally it is the result of bilateral hyperplasia of the zona glomerulosa.

What biochemical abnormalities does Conn's syndrome produce?

Conn's syndrome produces high plasma aldosterone and low renin levels. This results in a hypokalaemia and metabolic alkalosis.

APPLIED PHYSIOLOGY AND CRITICAL CARE

1. THE ACTION POTENTIAL

What is an action potential?

An action potential is a rapid change in the membrane potential followed by a return to the resting membrane potential. The size and shape of an action potential varies considerably between excitable tissues and is due to the differing populations of voltage dependent ion channels.

What tissues have an action potential?

The tissues which have an action potential include neurons and all types of muscle cell.

Can you draw an example of a neuron action potential?

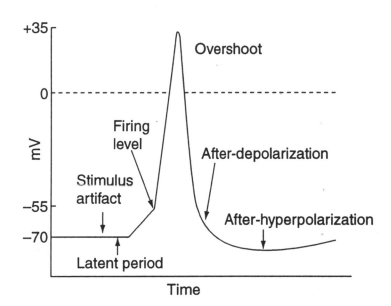

Can you describe the ionic events occurring during the action potential of a typical neuron?

- A typical neuron has a resting membrane potential of –70 mV. This is determined by the relative amounts of Na^+, K^+, and Cl^- inside and outside the cell.
- A local supra-threshold stimulus activates the fast Na^+ channels. This causes a rapid influx of Na^+ into the cell. This persists for less than 1 millisecond and causes a depolarisation of the membrane potential (i.e. the potential becomes closer to zero).
- The depolarisation overshoots the zero value to approximately + 30 mV. This inactivates the sodium channels and therefore stops the inward sodium current.
- The voltage dependent K^+ channels open, which together with the closed Na^+ channels result in a rapid repolarisation back to the resting membrane potential of –70 mV.
- During the inactivation of the Na^+ channels the cell is refractory to further stimulus

What determines the conduction velocity of an action potential?

Two factors determine action potential velocity

- **Diameter of the axon**, large cells have a faster conduction velocity
- **Myelination** increases velocity because the action potential is propagated from one node of Ranvier to the next because the intervening membrane is non-excitable and cannot fire an action potential. This jumping of potential from node to node is termed saltatory conduction. (A node of Ranvier is the gap between two adjacent Schwann cells.)

What affects the magnitude of the action potential along the length of a neuron?

The action potential is an all or nothing phenomenon. It has the same magnitude along the entire length of the neuron. Information is therefore coded in terms of frequency of impulses.

Can you draw an example of a cardiac muscle action potential?

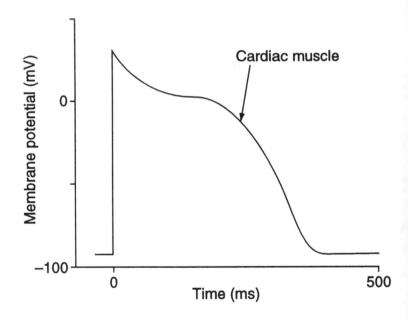

What is the difference between the action potential of a neuron and cardiac muscle?

Cardiac muscle cells have an additional voltage channel which creates the characteristic cardiac muscle action potential. This is the slow Ca^{2+} channel. This channel opens and the muscle is depolarised. It maintains the depolarised state so creating a plateau phase. During this phase, contraction is stimulated by release of more Ca^{2+} from the sarcoplasmic reticulum. The cell is also refractory to further stimulus during this phase and therefore tetany is not possible.

2.   METABOLIC RESPONSE TO SURGERY

What is the body's response to 1 litre haemorrhage?

1 litre of blood loss equates to class 2 hypovolaemic shock. This produces mild anxiety in the patient, a tachycardia (pulse rate is >100 bpm), decreased pulse pressure but a normal blood pressure. The respiratory rate increases to 20–30 breaths per minute and the urine output falls slightly (20–30 ml/hr).

What is the endocrine response to trauma?

The endocrine response to trauma is widespread. The responses include

- **Catecholamine** release from the adrenal medulla, which produces inotropic and chronotropic effects on the heart, peripheral vasoconstriction, increased gluconeogenesis and lipolysis
- **Cortisol** levels are increased leading to increased proteolysis, gluconeogenesis, lipolysis and acute phase proteins release
- **Aldosterone** release is also increased and causes increased renal sodium and water retention
- **Increased anti-diuretic hormone** release from the posterior pituitary causing increased water retention
- Other endocrine responses include increased **glucagon** secretion (leading to increased glycogenolysis and gluconeogenesis), and a **fall in insulin** secretion. **Growth hormone** release is increased, this elevates hepatic glucose output and decreases glucose uptake by tissues.

What happens to glucose metabolism in trauma?

Immediately after injury, plasma glucose levels rise as a result of increased sympathetic outflow and circulating catecholamines. The body's glycogen store is soon depleted. However, glucose levels are maintained by the breakdown of protein and fat.

Recycling of lactate produced by anaerobic respiration in the liver also produces glucose. Other factors which serve to maintain an elevated blood glucose include glucagon and corticosteroid secretion.

What are the effects of trauma on protein metabolism?

Protein metabolism is disturbed in the flow phase of injury. The degree of disturbance is **proportional to the magnitude of injury** and the nutritional status of the patient, so the more severe the injury, the greater the rate of synthesis and breakdown of protein. Malnutrition itself tends to depress synthesis. Following major trauma, approximately 20% of the body's protein store is lost in the first three weeks (mostly during the first 10 days). Two-thirds of this loss is from skeletal muscle.

Which amino acids are particularly lost from skeletal muscle breakdown?

Two amino acids, **alanine** and **glutamine** account for approximately 60% of the nitrogen released from the breakdown of skeletal muscle protein.

What is the role of these two amino acids?

Glutamine is a primary energy source for immune cells and enterocytes. Alanine is a major source for gluconeogenesis.

Can you describe the effects of trauma on lipid metabolism?

Following trauma, there is increased production of free fatty acids and glycerol from triglycerides. This is mainly stimulated by beta-adrenergic mechanisms, although glucagon, cortisol and growth hormone all make some contribution. Free fatty acids act as a source of energy as they may be oxidised in both cardiac and skeletal muscle. In addition, glycerol contributes to gluconeogenesis.

What do you understand by the ebb phase of the response to injury?

The **ebb phase** is the early acute response to injury and is seen in the first 12–24 hours. It is characterised by the mobilisation of energy reserves and changes in cardiovascular activity. The changes which are seen during the ebb phase include changes in homeostatic reflex activity (thermoregulatory and cardiovascular).

The patient

- is cold and clammy with poor tissue perfusion
- has a low cardiac output
- has a low core temperature
- is hypometabolic with lowered energy expenditure
- has mild protein catabolism
- has elevated blood glucose, elevated catecholamines, elevated glucocorticoids and glucagon levels
- has low insulin levels

What do you understand by the flow phase of the response to injury?

The **flow phase of the response to injury** signifies a period of increased metabolic rate and increased urinary nitrate secretion. It is associated with weight loss and muscle wasting, reaching a maximum of 7–10 days after injury. However, this may be prolonged to many weeks if there is multiple organ failure or sepsis.

The patient in the flow phase of response to injury is warm and pink with normal tissue perfusion. There is evidence of

- Hypermetabolism
- Raised core temperature
- Increased energy expenditure
- Increased glucose production
- Profound protein catabolism
- Elevated glucose, catecholamines, glucocorticoids, insulin and glucagon levels

3. ACID–BASE DISTURBANCES

What is the normal pH range in the blood?

The normal pH range is 7.35–7.45.

Why is the pH maintained within such a narrow range?

The purpose of regulating the pH within this narrow range is to maintain the shape and structure of enzymes which control numerous metabolic reactions in the body. Failure of regulation leads to cellular damage.

How is this pH maintained?

Any pH changes are buffered to minimise any immediate effects. The kidneys and lungs are then involved in further modification through the excretion of 'acid'.

What is the main buffer system in the extracellular fluid?

The **CO_2/HCO_3^- buffer** is the most important system in the body.

$$CO_2 + H_2O \overset{CA}{\Leftrightarrow} H_2CO_3 \Leftrightarrow H^+ + HCO_3^-$$

Carbonic anhydrase (CA) catalyses the first (rate limiting) step. The second step is instantaneous.

How is acid produced in normal metabolism?

Two forms of 'acid' are produced in normal metabolism. Metabolism of carbohydrates and fats produce CO_2 which is called a **'volatile' acid** because it can be excreted from the lungs. The metabolism of many foods, particularly those that have a high protein content produce **'non-volatile' acids** such as sulphuric, hydrochloric and phosphoric acid.

What do you understand by the term metabolic acidosis?

Metabolic acidosis is the condition where the plasma pH falls below 7.35 following a decrease in the plasma HCO_3^-.

What are the common causes of metabolic acidosis?

The commonest cause of metabolic acidosis is anaerobic metabolism secondary to poor oxygen delivery to the tissues. Thus, metabolic acidosis commonly occurs following cardiogenic shock (post-MI), hypovolaemia (trauma, septic shock) or in situations of increased oxygen demand (sepsis, trauma).

How would you interpret these arterial blood gases? pH 7.30, HCO_3^- 18 mmol/l (normal 23–25 mmol/l); pCO_2 30 mmHg (normal = 40 mmHg)

The pH is <7.35 so this represents an acidosis. To determine whether this is a metabolic or respiratory acidosis we must look at the pCO_2 and HCO_3^-. The pCO_2 here is low, so a respiratory acidosis may be excluded. Therefore, the only other condition that this could be is a metabolic acidosis. This is also suggested by the fact that the HCO_3^- is low. As the fall in pH is secondary to a low HCO_3^-, the lungs compensate by increasing the excretion of CO_2 (thus pCO_2 falls).

4.   THE KIDNEY

What are the functions of the kidney?

The important functions of the kidney include

- **Maintenance of body fluid osmolality and volume**, electrolyte and **acid-base balance**. Osmolality is regulated by the excretion of water and NaCl. Acid-base balance is achieved through secretion of H^+ and absorption of HCO_3^-.

- **Elimination** of water-soluble waste products of metabolism and foreign substances. Metabolic products include urea (from amino acids) and creatinine (from muscle protein). Foreign substances include breakdown products of drugs.

- **Hormone production** and secretion. Hormones include

  - Renin
  - 1,25 dihydroxycholecalciferol
  - Erythropoietin
  - Prostaglandins and kinins (such as bradykinin)

How does the kidney maintain a constant extracellular fluid (ECF) osmolality?

NaCl is the major determinant of ECF osmolality. Large variations of water and NaCl ingestion do not produce similar changes in ECF volume and osmolality, as the kidney is able to compensate by excreting urine that is either hyperosmotic (concentrated) or hypo-osmotic (dilute) with respect to the ECF.

If ECF osmolality increases, the hypothalamus responds by increasing anti-diuretic hormone (ADH) release. ADH increases the permeability of the collecting ducts of the kidney to water. Water is thus reabsorbed resulting in a small volume of concentrated urine.

If the ECF osmolality decreases, ADH secretion and the sensation of thirst are both suppressed. This results in reduced water reabsorption from the collecting ducts and production of a large volume of dilute urine.

How is ECF volume regulated?

The ECF volume is regulated by low and **high pressure sensors**. Baroreceptors (pressure sensors) in the aortic arch, carotid sinus and afferent arterioles of the kidneys send afferent impulses to the brain stem via the vagus and glossopharyngeal nerves about the ECF volume. For example if ECF volume rises, there is decreased sympathetic activity and reduced ADH secretion. In addition, pressure receptors in the afferent arterioles of the kidney suppress renin secretion through a negative feed back loop. The net result is systemic vasodilatation and decreased renal Na^+ absorption.

Low pressure sensors (pulmonary vessels and atria) have the opposite effect so that sympathetic activity, ADH secretion and the Renin-Angiotensin-Aldosterone axis are all stimulated.

What are the indications for dialysis or haemofiltration?

The indications are

- Symptoms of uraemia
- Complications of uraemia e.g. pericarditis
- Severe biochemical derangement in the absence of symptoms (e.g. rising trend in an oliguric patient)
- Hyperkalaemia not controlled by conservative measures
- Severe acidosis
- Removal of drugs causing acute renal failure (gentamicin, lithium, aspirin overdose)

5. ACUTE RENAL FAILURE

How would you define acute renal failure?

Acute renal failure in adults may be defined as a creatinine >125 µmol/l recorded within the last 48 hours and oliguria of <135 ml in the last 8 hours.

In practice what should the normal urinary output be above?

0.5 ml/kg per hour.

What does the picture of oliguria and high urine osmolality indicate?

This indicates that the kidneys are concentrating urine appropriately and indicates a pre-renal cause for the oliguria. If you have oliguria and a urine osmolality similar to serum osmolality, i.e. 300 µmol/l, this suggests established renal failure.

Can renal failure occur without oliguria?

Yes, particularly if diuretics are used to maintain urine flow.

What are the common causes of acute renal failure in a surgical patient?

The common causes of acute renal failure in surgical patients are sepsis and hypotension.

Can you list any risk factors that predispose a surgical patient to developing post-op acute renal failure?

The potential risk factors are pre-existing renal disease, diabetes mellitus, pre-existing cardiac failure, evidence of reno-vascular disease and hypertension. The older patient is also more prone to developing renal failure. Diuretics, antibiotics such as amino-glycosides (gentamicin), non-steroidal anti-inflammatory agents, cyclosporin and contrast media will exacerbate renal failure. In addition, jaundice or myoglobinaemia will have detrimental effects on the kidneys.

Can you outline the principles of management of acute renal failure?

The management of acute renal failure is not restricted to the kidneys but the management of the patient as a whole. It is important to treat any multiple organ dysfunction.

The patient should be resuscitated. Hypoperfusion must be corrected, with the use of fluids, blood and inotropes as necessary. Invasive cardiovascular monitoring may be of advantage depending on the patient's condition. Treatment of any underlying sepsis should be commenced. Appropriate antibiotics must be given having adjusted for reduced excretion rates due to renal failure. Nutritional support should also be considered.

Are diuretics of any use in the treatment of acute renal failure?

Diuretics may be useful in some patients to maintain urine volume. However, if they are used inappropriately they may precipitate acute renal failure. Furosemide has theoretical benefit in that it may reduce medullary work thereby reducing tubular oxygen demand. Furosemide acts on the loop of Henlé and reduces chloride and hence sodium re-absorption. Some studies have shown that a continuous infusion of Furosemide rather than boluses is more beneficial, as bolusing may induce further hypovolaemia.

Mannitol has also been used and is often described as a renal protective agent due to its osmotic-diuretic, free-radical scavenger and renal vasodilatory effects. However, prospective trials have not demonstrated any clear benefit. It is of great importance when considering using diuretics in patients with acute renal failure to ensure that cardiovascular resuscitation and fluid loading has been performed before instituting diuretic treatment.

6. FLUIDS

How would you classify the fluid compartments in the body?

The body fluid compartments can be divided into extra-cellular and intra-cellular. The intra-cellular fluid compartment accounts for two-thirds of the total body water. The extra-cellular fluid compartment includes the intra-vascular volume and the interstitial fluid volume. In a 70 kg man, the intra-cellular fluid accounts for 28 litres, the extra-cellular fluid 11 litres and the plasma volume 3 litres.

What is the volume and composition of the body fluids?

Volumes and Electrolyte Content of Body Fluids.

	Volume (ml/day)	Sodium (mmol/l)	Potassium (mmol/l)	Chloride (mmol/l)	Bicarbonate (mmol/l)
Saliva	1500	30	20	35	15
Stomach	2000	50	10	150	0
Pancreas	1000	140	5	30	120
Bile	1500	140	5	100	30
Small bowel	3500	100	5	100	25
Large bowel	500	80	15	50	0
Sweat	0-500	50	10	50	0
Diarrhoea	variable	80	30	60	25

Can you describe how 1 litre of 0.9% normal saline is distributed when infused into a patient?

Following infusion, only 25% of Normal saline stays in the intravascular space. The remaining 75% redistributes into the interstitial space, hence only 250 ml is 'added' to the plasma volume.

How does this compare to infusing 1 litre of 5% dextrose?

In the case of infusing 5% dextrose, only 8% remains in the plasma and 92% redistributes into the interstitial and intracellular compartments. So for 1 litre of 5% dextrose, only 80 ml is 'added' to the plasma volume.

How do colloids differ from crystalloids?

Colloids are fluids which exert an oncotic pressure either via protein particles (**natural colloids**) or via synthetic particles (**artificial colloids**). Crystalloids have approximately the same composition and osmolality of plasma, and rapidly redistribute throughout the extra-cellular fluid compartments. Plasma expanders have a high concentration of osmotically active particles so that there is a shift of fluid from the interstitial tissue to the intra-vascular space.

What colloid solutions do you know?

Colloids solutions can be classified into **natural and synthetic solutions**. The natural solutions include fresh frozen plasma, purified protein fraction, human albumin and plasma protein solutions. The synthetic or artificial colloids include the gelatins, hydroxy ethyl starch and dextrans.

Do the colloids interfere with cross-matching?

Gelatins such as haemaccel and gelofusin do not interfere with cross matching or haemostasis. However, dextrans such as dextran 40 and dextran 70 are commonly associated with coagulation abnormalities and interfere with blood cross matching. The hydroxy ethyl starch solutions such as hetastarch and pentastarch may interfere with haemostasis if large volumes are transfused (dilutional coagulopathy).

What do you understand by the term third space fluid loss?

Third space fluid loss is the sequestration of sodium rich fluid into the interstitial space as a result of infection, inflammation or tissue trauma.

7. OXYGEN CARRIAGE AND DISSOCIATION

Can you draw the Hb-oxygen dissociation curve and label the important values?

Curve of Oxygen saturation (%) versus pO_2 (mmHg).

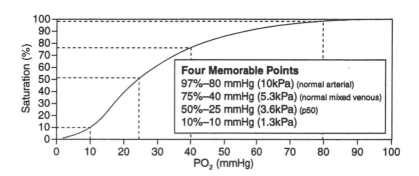

Important points on the curve:

- The normal oxygen saturation of arterial blood is 98% when the p_aO_2 is 100 mmHg
- The normal oxygen saturation of venous blood is 75% when the p_aO_2 is 40 mmHg
- At a pO_2 of 26 mmHg, under normal physiological conditions, the saturation of Hb is 50%

What is the physiological advantage of a sigmoid shaped curve?

A sigmoid shaped curve maximises the quantity of oxygen taken up in the lungs at low alveolar oxygen tension but maximises the quantity released in the systemic capillaries at a relatively high partial pressure.

What is the effect of a right shift in the oxygen dissociation curve?

A shift of the curve to the right decreases the affinity of oxygen for Hb i.e. oxygen is released more readily from Hb at a given pO_2. Therefore, at a given partial pressure of oxygen, say 26 mmHg, the standard Hb-oxygen dissociation curve has a saturation of 50% which is reduced to 40% with a small right shift.

Can you tell me what produces a right shift of the oxygen dissociation curve?

The causes include

- ↑ temperature
- High pCO_2 (the right shift in the curve secondary to a high pCO_2 is termed the Bohr effect)
- ↑ concentration of H^+
- ↑ concentration of 2,3-DPG (2,3-DPG is a product of anaerobic metabolism)

What happens to the oxygen dissociation curve in anaemia?

Anaemia reduces the overall oxygen carrying capacity of the blood but does not affect the percentage saturation of Hb, therefore the curve is unchanged.

How is CO_2 carried in the blood?

CO_2 is transported in the blood by three means

- The main mechanism is through the HCO_3^- buffer system which accounts for approximately 60% of CO_2 carriage
- Carbamino haemoglobin compounds account for approximately 30% of carriage of CO_2. CO_2 reacts with the amine groups in haemoglobin to form carbamino Hb. This reaction is faster if the Hb is deoxygenated, as in venous blood.
- The final mechanism is through dissolved CO_2. CO_2 is 20 times more soluble in blood than oxygen. This represents approximately 10% of the total CO_2 carriage.

What is the alveolar gas equation?

The alveolar gas equation describes the relationship between alveolar ventilation and p_aCO_2.

It is the p_aCO_2 that is constantly 'sensed' by the brain stem respiratory centre and used to regulate alveolar ventilation.

The equation states that the product of alveolar ventilation and arterial p_aCO_2 is a constant at any given level of CO_2 production.

## 8.	RESPIRATORY FAILURE AND VENTILATION

What do you understand by respiratory failure?

Respiratory failure occurs when ventilation is unable to meet the required oxygen demand or when the CO_2 produced cannot be adequately removed. Respiratory failure may be classified into two types.

Type 1:
p_aO_2 (< 8 kPa), p_aCO_2 normal – ventilation-perfusion mismatch, pulmonary embolism, ARDS

Type 2:
p_aO_2 (< 8 kPa), p_aCO_2 (> 7 kPa) – Impaired gas exchange e.g. chest trauma, pneumothorax, head injury

How is breathing controlled?

Breathing is regulated by two mechanisms: Automatic and Voluntary.

Automatic regulation:
Controlled by the brain stem: sensory information is relayed to the brain stem from central chemoreceptors near the surface of the medulla (peripheral chemoreceptors in the carotid and aortic bodies) and proprioceptors in the lung, intercostal muscles and diaphragm.

Voluntary regulation:
The central chemoreceptors respond to changes in p_aCO_2. The peripheral chemoreceptors respond to changes in H^+ and O_2. The response to O_2 is only significant at low partial pressures (<70 mmHg).

When might you consider performing a tracheostomy in a ventilated patient?

One might consider performing a tracheostomy if there is prolonged endotracheal intubation (>7 days), failed trial of extubation (i.e. ventilator dependent) or for removal of bronchial secretions.

What are the criteria for extubation?

It is important to assess and consider the general condition of the patient before considering extubation.

Various criteria have been proposed:

- Respiratory rate <45 breaths/min
- Tidal volume 4–5 ml/kg
- Vital capacity 10–15 ml/kg
- pO_2 > 8 kPa on 40% Oxygen
- pH > 7.3

- Stable cardiovascular system
- No severe abdominal distension
- No major metabolic disturbances
- Co-operative patient

If the ratio of <u>Respiratory rate: Tidal volume</u> is <80, this usually indicates a successful extubation.

What are the hazards of ventilation?

The hazards include

- Barotrauma including pneumothorax and pneumomediastinum
- Air embolus
- Subcutaneous emphysema
- Decreased cardiac output
- Nosocomial pneumonia
- Parenchymal lung damage

9.   CONTROL OF RESPIRATION

Where is the respiratory centre?

The respiratory centre is formed by two groups of neurons in the medulla near the floor of the IV ventricle. The dorsal group contains mostly inspiratory neurons and the ventral group, expiratory and inspiratory nuclei.

What factors control breathing?

Non-chemical and chemical factors are thought to have an important influence on the control of breathing:

*   The **cortex** (impulses from higher centres may be important in increasing ventilation in voluntary exercise)
*   Proprioceptive impulses from the **muscles of respiration**
*   **Blood pCO_2 and pH**. Respiration is finely regulated by p_aCO_2 levels (central chemo-receptors) which when increased stimulates ventilation. A fall in blood pH also stimulates ventilation.
*   **Hypoxia** itself stimulates breathing indirectly via the **aortic and carotid body** receptors. It does not have a direct effect on the chemoreceptors of the reticular formation.

What factors govern respiratory gas exchange in the lungs?

Respiratory gas exchange in the lungs depends on three factors – ventilation, diffusion and pulmonary capillary blood flow.

*   **Ventilation** involves the volume and distribution of the inspired air which ventilates the alveoli
*   **Diffusion** involves the passage of gases between the alveoli and blood in the alveolar capillaries
*   **Pulmonary capillary blood flow** involves the total volume of blood and its distribution to all the ventilated alveoli

What is the anatomical deadspace?

volume of the space in the respiratory system besides alveoli and other closely related gas exchange areas.

The anatomical deadspace is defined as the **volume of gas exhaled before the CO_2 concentration rises to its alveolar plateau**.

The volume of the anatomical deadspace is not constant and is influenced by many factors, including size of the subject, posture, position of the neck and jaw, age and the lung volume at the end of inspiration. Other factors include hypoventilation, hypothermia and drugs.

What is the physiological deadspace?

The physiological deadspace is defined as the **sum of all the parts of the tidal volume which do not participate in gaseous exchange**.

The physiological deadspace volume varies according to age, sex, body size, posture, duration of inspiration and breath-holding. It is well known that prolongation of inspiration reduces the deadspace, allowing gas mixing to take place between deadspace and alveolar gas.

What effects does general anaesthesia have on the respiratory system?

General anaesthesia produces a rise in p_aCO_2 due to a direct depressant effect of anaesthetic agents on the brain. In the post-operative period, there may be partial collapse of the small airways, resulting in a reduced ventilation-perfusion ratio, so leading to segmental collapse.

General anaesthesia may also cause increased sputum production, impairment of the cough reflex and reduced ciliary action. Aspiration may occur during or after anaesthesia, so causing respiratory distress.

10. ACUTE RESPIRATORY DISTRESS SYNDROME (ARDS)

How would you define acute respiratory distress syndrome (ARDS)?

The definition of ARDS remains controversial and the term ARDS should be reserved for those patients at the severe end of an 'acute lung injury' spectrum. ARDS may be defined as diffuse pulmonary infiltrates, refractory hypoxaemia, stiff lungs and respiratory distress following a recognised precipitating cause.

What are the criteria for diagnosing ARDS?

The criteria include the appropriate clinical setting with a history of a precipitating condition such as sepsis. On chest X-ray, bilateral infiltrates with no clinical evidence of clinical heart failure, fluid overload or chronic lung disease would be seen with

- Refractory hypoxaemia ($p_aO_2 < 8kPa$, $FiO_2 > 0.4$, $p_aO_2 / p_aO_2 < 0.25$)
- Pulmonary artery wedge pressure <18 mmHg
- $p_aO_2/FiO_2 < 200$ mmHg

What clinical conditions are commonly associated with the development of ARDS?

The most common conditions include

- Severe sepsis (50%)
- Trauma (30%)
- Gastric aspiration (10%)
- Other important causes include multiple trauma, fat embolus, massive blood transfusion and acute pancreatitis

What pathophysiological processes underlie ARDS?

The underlying processes are incompletely understood but a characteristic feature is diffuse alveolar-capillary damage. The disruption of the alveolar-capillary units can be divided into three phases: exudative, proliferative and fibrotic.

In the **exudative phase**, acute phase plasma proteins fill the alveoli, and endothelial injury is thought to be mediated by cytokines (TNFα, platelet activating factor and interleukins 1, 2, 6 and 8). Activated neutrophils also damage the endothelium by releasing proteolytic enzymes and oxygen radicals. This first phase lasts a few days and progresses into a proliferative phase.

In the **proliferative phase** there is activation and proliferation of type 2 pneumocytes and fibroblasts, which migrate into the alveolar space and produce granulation tissue and collagen. This results in remodelling of the pulmonary vasculature with occlusion of the vascular lumen.

In the **fibrotic phase** the lungs become scarred and further collagen is deposited.

How do you treat ARDS?

There is no specific therapy for ARDS and treatment remains supportive. Management treatment must be directed to the underlying cause of the respiratory failure/precipitating condition.

Management of ventilatory support is complex. Various strategies have been used including Positive End Expiratory Pressure (PEEP) using reversed I:E (Inspiration:Expiration/ventilation rations), small tidal volumes and permissive hypercapnia, prone positioning and inhaled nitric oxide.

11. CARDIAC OUTPUT

How is cardiac output regulated?

Cardiac output is regulated through factors that affect heart rate and stroke volume. These include

- **Neural** mechanisms: sympathetic, parasympathetic
- **Intrinsic** mechanisms to the heart: Starling's law of contractility (preload is proportional to cardiac output)
- **Hormonal** mechanisms: adrenaline, glucagon (less important), thyroxine

How can you measure the cardiac output?

A crude indication of cardiac output can be obtained clinically through peripheral skin temperature, BP, pulse, urine output and conscious level/state.

More direct and accurate methods include the insertion of a Doppler probe into the oesophagus to measure blood flow velocity in the descending aorta. A velocity time waveform is created and the total ventricular stroke volume can be calculated from the area under the waveform. From this, cardiac output may be determined.

A more precise method involves using a pulmonary artery catheter and the thermodilution method based on the Fick principle.

$$CO = HR \times SV$$
$$BP = CO \times SVR$$

(CO: Cardiac output; SV: Stroke volume; HR: Heart rate; BP: Blood pressure; SVR: Systemic vascular resistance.)

What is the Fick principle?

The Fick principle states that the amount of a substance taken up by an organ per unit of time is equal to the arterial level of the substance minus the venous level multiplied by the blood flow.

What can you use the Fick principle to calculate?

The Fick principle can be used to calculate blood flow (cardiac output) and CO_2 consumption.

What compensatory mechanisms are activated in severe haemorrhage?

Four interlinked mechanisms are activated following haemorrhage.

- Following haemorrhage there is a fall in mean arterial pressure and this produces a **baroreceptor response** (stretch receptors in the aortic arch and carotid sinus send afferents to the brain stem).

- Vagal (parasympathetic) tone is decreased resulting in ↑ Heart rate.
- The ↑ **in sympathetic tone** causes
  - Peripheral vasoconstriction leading to ↑ systemic vascular resistance
  - ↑ inotropic effect
  - ↑ chronotropic effect
  - ↑ stroke volume and thus cardiac output

There is ↓ **blood flow to the skin, skeletal muscle and splanchnic circulation**.

The **Renin-angiotensin-aldosterone axis** is also activated due to the fall in renal perfusion and glomerular filtration rate. This leads to arteriolar vasoconstriction and sodium retention, which increases plasma osmolarity and stimulates thirst and ADH release from the posterior pituitary leading to water retention.

12.   THE CARDIAC CYCLE

Can you draw the cardiac cycle?

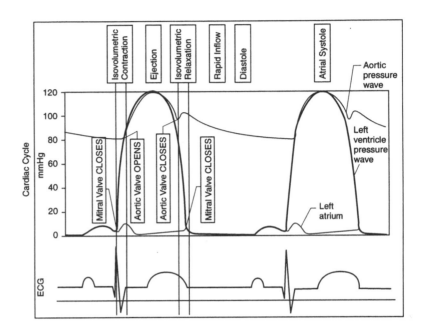

Pressure vs time axis; ECG trace; Atrial systole; mitral closes; ventricles contract; aortic valve opens; aortic valve closes; mitral valve opens; ventricular filling.

On an ECG, what do the p wave and QRS complex represent?

The **p wave** represents atrial depolarisation. Atrial systole begins shortly after the onset of the p wave.

The **QRS complex** represents ventricular depolarisation. Ventricular systole begins at the peak of the R wave and ends just after the T wave.

What does the dicrotic notch represent?

The dicrotic notch is seen on the descending limb of the aortic pressure curve and marks the division between ventricular systole and diastole. The aortic valve closes at this point.

Can you describe the opening and closing of the mitral valve in relation to the cardiac cycle?

The mitral valve closes at the end of atrial systole when the pressure in the left ventricle exceeds that of the left atrium. This marks the beginning of ventricular systole (the peak of the R wave).

The mitral valve opens in early ventricular diastole, when the pressure in the left ventricle is below that of the atrium. This is the end of isovolumetric relaxation of the ventricle. Opening of the mitral valve results in rapid ventricular filling.

Can you describe the opening and closing of the aortic valve in relation to the cardiac cycle?

The aortic valve opens in early ventricular systole when the pressure in the left ventricle exceeds that of the aorta (this marks the end of the period of isovolumetric contraction of the left ventricle - a short period at the start of ventricular systole when both the mitral and aortic valves are closed). The aortic valve closes when the pressure in the aorta is greater than the left ventricle. This marks the end of ventricular systole.

13.   BLOOD FLOW DYNAMICS

What are the resistance vessels?

The arterioles are the main resistance vessels in the body. They offer the greatest resistance to the flow of blood pumped by the heart. The main component of their walls is smooth muscle which is sensitive to a variety of factors, such as nitric oxide which reduces vascular tone and increases luminal diameter, and hence decreases resistance to flow.

What is the importance of these resistance vessels?

These vessels provide a mechanism for controlling the systemic vascular resistance (SVR) and therefore the blood pressure (BP). (BP = Cardiac Output x SVR.) Thus, these vessels influence perfusion to all parts of the body.

How are these resistance vessels regulated?

These resistance vessels are regulated by both neural and metabolic factors.

Neural regulation is predominantly through the sympathetic vasoconstrictor fibres to the blood vessels.

Metabolic regulation is achieved by vasodilator metabolites produced locally by the tissue when metabolically active or during anaerobic conditions. The metabolic factors producing vasodilatation include CO_2, H^+, K^+, adenosine and nitric oxide.

What processes are involved in controlling the movement of fluids across the capillary bed?

The movement of water and small solutes across the capillary endothelial wall occurs by three processes: **diffusion**, **filtration** and **absorption**.

The relationship between filtration and absorption is dependent on **Starling's forces**. The principal force in capillary filtration is the capillary hydrostatic pressure.

The main force that prevents fluid loss from the capillaries is the osmotic pressure of the plasma proteins otherwise known as the **colloid osmotic or oncotic pressure**. The capillary filtration pressure is the capillary hydrostatic pressure minus the interstitial hydrostatic pressure. The hydrostatic pressure within the capillaries is regulated by the arterial pressure, venous pressure and the resistance of the arterioles.

What influences the coronary artery blood flow?

Coronary artery blood flow is influenced by a combination of physical, metabolic and neural factors.

Physical factors: The main ones are aortic pressure, myocardial rate and contractility. Aortic pressure plays a primary role in determining myocardial perfusion. Aortic pressure itself is dependent on heart rate and stroke volume. Thus, during early diastole coronary inflow is maximal, and minimal during early ventricular systole.

Metabolic factors: Myocardial metabolic activity closely parallels coronary blood flow (this relationship is preserved in the denervated heart). Increased myocardial oxygen demand stimulates the release of vasodilator substances from the myocardium into the interstitial fluid causing relaxation of the coronary vessels and so increasing blood flow.

Neural factors: The direct neural influence on coronary blood flow is through the sympathetic nervous system (β1 receptors). However, stimulation of the sympathetic nervous system itself causes release of circulating catecholamines thereby increasing heart rate and contractility (β2 receptors) and so influences coronary blood flow indirectly.

How is the cerebral circulation regulated?

The cerebral circulation is regulated by physical (main influence), metabolic and neural factors.

Physical factors: The cranium should be considered a rigid, fixed box, so increases in the volume of blood, extracellular fluid, cerebrospinal fluid or cellular material (a tumour for example) would increase the intracranial pressure (ICP). (Cerebral perfusion pressure (CPP) = mean arterial pressure (MAP) − ICP). Cerebral blood flow itself is autoregulated between a certain range, thus blood flow is kept relatively constant despite changes in the CPP). The changes in blood volume are influenced by changes in arteriolar diameter which are in turn affected by the p_aCO_2 level.

Metabolic factors: cerebral blood flow is autoregulated so that total cerebral blood flow is constant. However, regional cortical blood flow is also related to local cortical activity. This is influenced by metabolic factors, especially carbon dioxide, potassium, adenosine and hydrogen ions. High levels of these metabolites cause vasodilation and increased blood flow.

Neural factors: the cerebral vessels receive a sympathetic supply but their influence in regulating blood flow is minimal.

How is the cerebral circulation affected by changes in ventilation?

Ventilation produces its main effect on the cerebral circulation through changes in arterial p_aCO_2 levels. Hyperventilation decreases p_aCO_2 levels causing cerebral vasoconstriction with a subsequent lowering of ICP.

Aim for low-normal CO_2 conc.

This technique is used to reduce the ICP in patients with head injury. The lowered ICP helps to maintain the CPP and reduce cerebral ischaemia.

14. CARDIOVASCULAR MONITORING

How is the Central Venous Pressure (CVP) measured?

CVP may be assessed clinically by looking for the jugular venous waveform. In a normal healthy person, reclining at 45°, the manubriosternal joint (the angle of Louis) may be up to 5 cm above the right atrium. Thus, the venous waveform either may or may not be just visible above the clavicle.

The CVP may also be measured by invasive means, by inserting a central line into the right atrium usually via the subclavian or internal jugular vein. Other routes include via the cephalic and femoral veins.

What is a normal range for the CVP?

The normal range is 0–10 mmHg (1–13 cm H_2O). The reference point (zero point) is the surface marking of the right atrium. This equates to the mid-axillary line if the patient is lying flat.
The range is dependent on the function of the right side of the heart. The actual numerical measurement of CVP pressure is less useful than its response to fluid bolus challenging.

What are the complications of a CVP line?

The complications may be divided into early and late.

Early complications are related to insertion and include haematoma, haemorrhage, air embolus and pneumothorax.

Late complications include thrombophlebitis and catheter infection.

What does the CVP tell us about the heart?

The CVP only gives information about the filling pressure of the right atrium.

In diastole, this filling pressure in the heart is called the preload. The preload causes the ventricular muscle to stretch and this is proportional to the force of contraction according to Starling's law. Thus, an increased force of contraction will increase the cardiac output. The relationship between the CVP and force of contraction only applies if there is no intrinsic lung disease or right heart pathology (e.g. valvular disease or cor pulmonale).

Arterial resistance is only indirectly proportional to the CVP so we cannot use the CVP alone to predict the cardiac output. The most useful clinical application of CVP measurement is to monitor the change in the CVP following a fluid challenge or inotrope administration.

What can a pulmonary artery catheter measure?

Pressure measurements can be taken from the central veins, right atrium, right ventricle and pulmonary artery as the catheter is floated through these structures. When the balloon is wedged in one of the pulmonary arteries measurement of the left atrial pressure may be taken.

In addition, one can measure cardiac output using a thermodilution technique based on the modified Fick principle.

Can you describe the principles of the thermodilution technique to measure cardiac output?

The technique involves injecting a known volume and temperature of cold normal saline into the right atrium. The saline mixes with the blood in the right atrium and ventricle and passes into the pulmonary artery where the fall in temperature is detected, thus causing a drop in temperature which is proportional to the cardiac output (dilution curve). From these measurements, one can calculate systemic vascular resistance and oxygen delivery.

What are the indications for inserting a pulmonary artery catheter?

The precise indications are not clearly defined and vary according to intensive care units but in principle it may be of use

- Where there is great difficulty with managing fluid replacement, especially in patients in whom cardiac function is also compromised (e.g. cardiogenic or septic shock).
- Where oxygen supply and demand need to be more precisely defined.

What are the complications of inserting a pulmonary artery catheter?

In addition to the complications of inserting a CVP line

- Dysrhythmias during insertion
- Rupture of the pulmonary artery (due to prolonged inflation of balloon)
- Pulmonary infarction
- Valvular damage
- Catheter knotting
- Mortality of 2%

15.   ITU AND SHOCK

Which sort of patient would you consider admitting to an intensive care unit?

- Patients requiring or who are likely to require advanced respiratory support
- Patients requiring support to two or more organ systems
- Patients who have chronic impairment of one or more organ systems and who also require support for acute reversible failure of another organ.

What factors need to be considered when assessing suitability for admission to intensive care?

The diagnosis, age, severity of the illness, co-existing disease, prognosis, availability of suitable treatment, response to treatment, anticipated quality of life and patient's wishes.

What clinical signs are suggestive of poor tissue perfusion?

Confusion, diminishing conscious level, tachycardia, cool cyanosed extremities, poor capillary refill, poor peripheral pulses, poor urine output (less than 0.5 ml/kg per hour), metabolic acidosis and rising blood lactate concentration.

How would you define shock?

Shock can be defined as the acute circulatory failure with inadequate and inappropriately distributed tissue perfusion resulting in generalised cellular hypoxia.

What is the difference between the systemic inflammatory response syndrome and septic shock?

The systemic inflammatory response syndrome is a systemic response to endothelial inflammation and is defined by the presence of two or more of the clinical signs of a temperature >38°C or less than <36°C, heart rate >90 bpm, the presence of tachypnoea or a white cell count >12 x 10^9/l or <4 x 10^9/l or the presence of more than 10% immature neutrophils.

In contrast, septic shock is sepsis induced hypotension despite adequate fluid resuscitation. Hence, it is a haemodynamic disturbance characterised by raised cardiac output and reduced systemic vascular resistance.

16.   PHYSIOLOGICAL EFFECTS OF ALTITUDE AND DIVING

What are the main physiological effects of altitude?

The physiological effects include

- Hypoxia $\rightarrow$ hyperventilation $\rightarrow$ low p_aCO_2
- Rise in cerebral blood flow $\rightarrow$ cerebral oedema
- Low O_2 $\rightarrow$ pulmonary vasoconstriction $\rightarrow$ pulmonary hypertension $\rightarrow$ pulmonary oedema

As one ascends to high altitude, the first effect is a fall in p_aO_2. This hypoxaemia stimulates a number of compensatory mechanisms. Hyperventilation is caused by stimulation of the peripheral chemoreceptors (mainly the carotid bodies). This causes the p_aCO_2 and $[H^+]$ to fall.

What physiological changes can be seen with acclimatisation?

Initially in the acclimatation process there is an increase in respiratory drive (hyperventilation).

Later

- Haemoglobin concentration increases which has the effect of increasing the oxygen carrying capacity
- 2,3 DPG (diphosphoglycerate) concentration rises, which in turn decreases the affinity of Hb for oxygen so causing a right shift of the O_2 dissociation curve

What are the main physiological effects of diving?

For every 10 m of depth in sea water, the ambient pressure increases by 1 atmosphere. The lung volume halves at a depth of 10 m and the partial pressures of the gases double. This may lead to nitrogen narcosis, oxygen toxicity, impairment of intellectual functions, tremors or drowsiness.

What are the main dangers of a fast ascent?

Barotrauma, air embolism and decompression sickness are the main dangers of a fast ascent. Nitrogen escapes from solution and bubbles in the tissues may cause severe pains (especially joints), neurological symptoms and in more severe cases the bubbles may obstruct the cerebral, pulmonary and coronary vessels.

17. EXOCRINE FUNCTION OF THE PANCREAS

What is the exocrine function of the pancreas?

The exocrine function of the pancreas is to produce digestive enzymes, fluid and electrolytes to modify and optimise the pH environment in the duodenum for enzyme reactions.

What enzymes does the pancreas synthesise?

The pancreas synthesises three main groups of enzymes. A proteolytic group which includes trypsinogen, chymotrypsinogen, procarboxypeptidases and proelastase. A lipolytic enzyme group consisting of lipase and phospholipase and finally the starch and polysaccharide enzymes (amylase).

What are their functions?

The proteolytic enzymes, of which trypsinogen is the most important, activate other proteolytic enzyme precursors through an autocatalytic process.

Pancreatic amylase hydrolyses starch, glycogen and other carbohydrates.

Pancreatic lipases hydrolyse and neutralise fat into fatty acids and triglycerides.

How is pancreatic secretion regulated?

Pancreatic secretion is regulated by two mechanisms: neural and hormonal.

Neural control occurs during the cephalic and gastric phases of digestion when the pancreas is stimulated by impulses along the vagus nerve to release pancreatic enzymes.

Hormonal regulation is the most important mechanism. It is mediated by hormones released from the mucosa when the chyme enters the duodenum.

Other factors which also play a role include direct stimulation of the acid in the cells by insulin and other gastrointestinal hormones such as **gastrin**.

Secretin is released when acid enters the duodenum and this causes the pancreatic ducts to secrete large amounts of fluid with a high bicarbonate content. The bicarbonate neutralises the acid and creates the necessary luminal pH for activity of the pancreatic enzymes. **Cholecystokinin** is the second important hormone involved in pancreatic secretion. It is released when food, particularly fatty acids, enters the duodenum. Cholecystokinin stimulates secretion of pancreatic juice.

What would be the effects of a total pancreatectomy on absorption?

Following a total pancreatectomy there would be reduced fat absorption leading to malabsorption of the fat soluble vitamins A, D and K. Other effects include reduced protein absorption and loss of normal glucose control with the development of a diabetic state.

18.   GASTRIC ACID SECRETION

What is the composition of gastric juice?

Gastric juice contains hydrochloric acid with up to 2 litres being secreted per day, together with pepsinogen and mucus.

What cells in the stomach are responsible for producing these substances?

Hydrochloric acid is produced by the parietal cells which are found primarily in the body of the stomach. Pepsinogen is produced by the chief cells and these are located in the body and antrum of the stomach. Mucus is produced by cells at the top of the gastric glands and are found throughout the stomach.

What controls gastric secretion?

The physiological regulation of gastric secretion can be divided into cephalic, gastric and intestinal phases.

- The cephalic phase is mediated by the vagus nerve (parasympathetic).
- The gastric phase is influenced primarily through local reflex responses and responses to gastrin.
- The intestinal phase is mediated through normal reflex and hormonal feedback initiated from the mucosa of the small intestine. It also involves secretin and cholecystokinin. Fats, carbohydrates and acid in the duodenum exert a negative feedback as they inhibit gastric acid and pepsin secretion.

What happens to gastric acid secretion when large parts of the small intestine are removed?

Gastric acid secretion is increased and the amount is roughly proportional to the amount of intestine removed.

Do you know of any other factors that may influence acid and pepsin secretion?

Hypoglycaemia can stimulate acid and pepsin secretion via cerebral and vagal influences. In addition, stimulants such as alcohol and coffee can act directly on the gastric mucosa.

19.   NUTRITION AND THE SURGICAL PATIENT

When should nutritional support be considered in a surgical patient?

Nutritional support should be considered in any patient who is unable to have an adequate dietary intake for more than 3 or 4 days.

What are the metabolic responses to fasting?

The metabolic responses include a fall in the insulin level and a rise in the plasma glucagon level (in an attempt to maintain an adequate level of glucose for the brain). Glycogen stores are also mobilised from the liver. In addition, there is breakdown of muscle and visceral protein, which produces the amino acids, alanine and glutamine which are precursors for hepatic gluconeogenesis. Breakdown of glycerol and triglycerides to produce fatty acids is also seen.

Catabolism.

What problems does malnutrition cause in a surgical patient?

The problems of malnutrition include

- Poor wound healing
- Gastromucosal atrophy
- Loss of muscle mass
- Reduced respiratory function
- Reduced immune function
- Reduced protein synthesis

Whether these problems translate into increased post-operative morbidity is debatable though, more recently, studies have shown benefit of pre-op feeding only in patients with severe malnutrition.

What methods of nutritional support are there?

Nutritional support may be either enteral or parenteral. If the gastrointestinal tract is working and access to it may be safely attained, then enteral feeding is the method of choice as it is cheaper, safer and has physiological advantages including prevention of bacterial translocation, gut mucosal atrophy, promotion of biliary flow and reduction of nosocomial pneumonia.

In what instances would enteral feeding be unsuitable?

Enteral feeding would be unsuitable in cases of complete small bowel obstruction, prolonged paralytic ileus with evidence of small bowel dilatation, severe diarrhoea and proximal small intestinal fistulae.

What are the complications of enteral feeding?

Complications of enteral feeding may be related to delivery of the nutrient to the gastrointestinal tract or related to intubation of the gastrointestinal tract. With regards to delivery, diarrhoea is the most common complication, occurring in 5–10% of patients. Aspiration and feed intolerance are two other well-known complications. Complications related to the intubation of the GI tract include blockage of the tube, displacement, wound infection, fistula formation and peritonitis.

What are the complications associated with TPN?

Complications associated with TPN may be related to insertion of the catheter and include **infective and mechanical problems**, namely

- Line sepsis
- Infective endocarditis
- Cannulation of the carotid artery
- Haematoma
- Migration
- Dislodgement
- Pneumothorax

Some of the **metabolic complications** include

- Hypo/hyperglycaemia
- Deranged liver function manifesting as abnormal liver function tests
- Hyperchloraemic acidosis
- Low phosphate
- High calcium
- High and low potassium levels
- High and low sodium levels in addition to deficiencies of trace elements, vitamins, essential fatty acids, folate, zinc and magnesium

These metabolic complications only occur in approximately 5% of patients.

'Refeeding syndrome' (can occur with enteral feeding as well) is a rare but well documented complication and is due to an over rapid shift of potassium and phosphate into the cells. It may manifest itself with cardiac arrest and death.

20.   LYMPHATICS

What is the function of the lymphatic system?

The function of the lymphatic system is to return plasma, capillary filtrate and protein to the vascular system. The lymphatic system also

- Filters the lymph nodes thereby removing foreign particles including bacteria
- Carries nutrients absorbed from the gastrointestinal tract including chylomicrons (fats) back to the circulation.

What is the difference between lymphatic and blood capillaries?

Lymphatic capillaries are similar to blood capillaries in many ways, but have two important differences. Firstly, tight junctions are not present between capillary endothelial cells, and secondly, fine filaments anchor lymph vessels to the surrounding connective tissue.

What tissues in the body do not contain lymphatic vessels?

Cartilage, bone, CNS tissue and epithelium do not contain lymphatic vessels.

What factors affect lymphatic flow?

Lymphatic flow is influenced by any mechanism that enhances the rate of capillary filtration. Thus, increased capillary pressure or capillary permeability or decreased plasma osmotic pressure all have an effect. Lymph flow also varies in proportion to the degree of muscular activity and is almost nil in resting skeletal muscle.

21.   IRON ABSORPTION AND TRANSPORT

What is the role of iron in the body?

Iron is an absolute requirement for the synthesis of haemoglobin, so its deficiency leads to hypochromic, microcytic anaemia.

What is the usual daily requirement of iron?

Approximately 25 mg of iron is required daily for haemopoiesis. The majority of iron in the body is recycled and only 1 mg of iron is absorbed per day. The normal diet contains between 10 and 25 mg a day.

How does iron deficiency occur?

Iron deficiency generally results from increased losses. Only in very rare instances does it occur as a result of failure of absorption or dietary deficiency.

Where is iron absorbed?

Iron absorption occurs in the upper small intestine.

How is it absorbed?

Absorption occurs when iron is in the reduced ferrous form (Fe^{2+}). Haem iron is also relatively well absorbed (20%).

In the epithelial cell, iron is split from the haem by the enzyme haemoxidase. Once Fe^{2+} enters the epithelial cell, it is bound to a cytosolic protein called mobilferrin at the basolateral membrane of the epithelial cells. Transferrin receptors mediate the transfer of the Fe^{2+} from mobilferrin to transferrin, and this Fe^{2+} transferrin complex is released into the extracellular fluid which then diffuses into the blood.

Where is iron stored?

Iron is stored in the liver, bone marrow and spleen, where it is stored as ferritin and haemosiderin.

22.   VITAMIN B$_{12}$

What is the function of vitamin B$_{12}$?

Vitamin B$_{12}$ is involved in the maturation of red blood cells and deficiency leads to **pernicious anaemia, subacute combined degeneration of the cord, irritation, depression** and **memory loss**.

Where is vitamin B$_{12}$ stored?

Vitamin B$_{12}$ is mainly stored in the **liver**, with a small amount present in the **bile**.

How long will the body store of vitamin B$_{12}$ last if absorption totally ceases?

The body's store of vitamin B$_{12}$ is very large and will last **3–6 years**.

Where is vitamin B$_{12}$ absorbed?

Vitamin B$_{12}$ is absorbed in the **distal ileum**.

Can you describe the mechanism by which vitamin B$_{12}$ is absorbed?

Following ingestion of food, pepsin in the stomach releases free vitamin B$_{12}$ from proteins. This free vitamin B$_{12}$ rapidly binds to a number of glycoproteins called R proteins.

During the intestinal phase of digestion, pancreatic proteases start to degrade the complexes between the R proteins and vitamin B$_{12}$. The free vitamin B$_{12}$, then rapidly binds to intrinsic factor which has been secreted by gastric parietal cells. Once bound this complex is taken up by the ileal epithelial cells and is slowly transported into the circulation.

Absorption of vitamin B$_{12}$ normally occurs in the presence of intrinsic factor. However, 1–2% occurs via intrinsic factor independent mechanisms.

What other substances are absorbed in the distal ileum?

The fat soluble **vitamins A, D, E and K and bile salts** are absorbed in the terminal ileum.

23.   CALCIUM HOMEOSTASIS

What is the approximate distribution of Ca^{2+} ions in the body?

99% bone, 0.9% intracellular, 0.1% extracellular. Approximately 40% of serum Ca^{2+} is protein bound.

How is serum Ca^{2+} concentration affected by pH?

The degree of protein binding and hence the amount of free unbound Ca^{2+} depends on the pH value of the blood. Alkalosis increases the level of protein binding whilst acidosis does the converse. Hence, hyperventilation causes tetany (hyperventilation decreases pCO$_2$ and therefore increases pH; resulting in increased protein binding of Ca^{2+} and lower free serum calcium Ca^{2+}).

How does Ca^{2+} influence the action potential?

Ca^{2+} influences the relationship between the membrane potential and Na$^+$ influx. A higher extracellular Ca^{2+} concentration stabilises the membrane by decreasing excitability. A lower Ca^{2+} concentration increases the exitability of nerve and muscle cells by decreasing the amount of depolarisation necessary to initiate the changes in Na$^+$ and K$^+$ flux that produce the action potential. Thus, muscular cramps and tetany are seen.

What are the clinical effects of a high Ca^{2+}?

- Muscle weakness
- Vomiting
- Nausea
- Renal calculi
- Cardiac arrhythmias
- Abdominal pain
- Dehydration
- Polyuria
- Renal failure
- Weight loss
- Corneal and vascular calcification
- Psychiatric disorders

"Bones, Stones and Abdominal Groans"

How is Ca^{2+} regulated?

Ca^{2+} balance is regulated by two main hormones: parathyroid hormone (PTH) and vitamin D. They act on three areas: intestine, kidneys and bones.

What is the body's response to a low Ca^{2+}?

The parathyroid glands monitor free ionised Ca^{2+} in the serum. PTH is secreted in response to a low Ca^{2+}. This hormone acts to increase Ca^{2+} by

- Increasing osteoclast activity on bone causing resorption of bone and release of Ca^{2+}
- Stimulating the kidneys to produce vitamin D which then

- acts on the intestine to increase absorption
- Stimulating the kidneys to absorb more Ca^{2+} from the urine. It also inhibits absorption of phosphate and prevents deposition of calcium phosphate.

How is vitamin D formed and what are its metabolites?

There are two sources of vitamin D: that produced in the skin by UV light (vitamin D_3) and that ingested in the diet (vitamin D_2). Both D_2 and D_3 have identical biological actions and so both forms are known as vitamin D. The active metabolites of vitamin D are produced by the 25-hydroxylation step in the liver (forming 25 hydroxy cholecalciferol) and 1α hydroxylation in the kidney (forming 1,25 DHCC or 1,25 dihydroxycholecalciferol). The 1,25 DHCC is the most active metabolite of vitamin D and is almost entirely responsible for the actions of vitamin D.

What is the role of Vitamin D?

Vitamin D acts on the intestine to increase Ca^{2+} and phosphate absorption and skeletal mineralisation. It also acts on bone, stimulating osteoclastic resorption. Hence, Vitamin D deficiency results in the formation of unmineralised osteoid. In children, this will affect the bony growth plates resulting in bowing of the extremities and collapse of the chest wall (rickets). In adults, bone pain, vertebral collapse and stress fractures will ensue (osteomalacia).

What are the possible causes of vitamin D deficiency?

- Insufficient sunlight exposure to the skin of individuals who have a diet poor in vitamin D
- Liver disease (affects the 25 hydroxylation step)
- Renal failure (affects the 1α hydroxylation step and hence production of the most active metabolite 1,25 DHCC)

24.   THERMOREGULATION

Where is the thermoregulatory centre considered to be?

The thermoregulatory centre is situated in the pre-optic region and the anterior hypothalamus.

The body has central and peripheral receptors.

What mechanisms are involved in the maintenance of body temperature?

Central receptors monitor core temperature, whereas the **peripheral receptors** consist of warm and cold receptors whose discharge increases with increasing and falling temperature respectively. The peripheral receptors enable the body to anticipate changes in core temperature. Additional sensory information also reaches cortical centres.

The other mechanisms involved in the control and maintenance of temperature, include

*   Control of skin blood flow
*   Venous circulation
*   Shivering and sweating

Skin blood flow is largely controlled by the sympathetic nervous system. Body cooling increases sympathetic tone inducing vasoconstriction, whilst warming inhibits the sympathetic system causing vasodilatation.

Control of the venous circulation is also an important mechanism in regulating heat loss from the skin. A combination of the large surface area of the veins and slow blood flow facilitates heat loss from the skin. Conversely, in cooler conditions, blood is shunted away from the superficial veins and is returned through the deep veins. In the limbs this may form a countercurrent heat exchanger with the arteries.

Shivering is a response to the cold and consists of bursts of involuntary unco-ordinated muscle contractions, which perform little mechanical work. As a result most of the metabolic energy appears as heat.

Heat may also be lost through the production of sweat and subsequent evaporatory loss. Sweating occurs when vasodilatation cannot provide sufficient heat loss to balance the body's heat gain.

What is sweat?

Sweat is a hypotonic solution containing approximately 60 mmol of sodium chloride.

What controls its production?

Its secretion is stimulated by the sympathetic system.
Acetylcholine is the neurotransmitter.

How much sweat can one produce?

Up to 1.5l of sweat may be secreted in one hour, but this may be rise to 4l per hour in a heat acclimatised subject.

What physiological changes occur following acclimatisation in a hot climate?

Following acclimatisation there is

- Increased rate of sweating
- Decreased core temperature
- Decreased heart rate
- Expansion of plasma volume
- Decreased sodium content of sweat

What hormonal changes are seen following changes in temperature?

In the cold, the adrenal medulla is stimulated so releasing catecholamines into the circulation. There is also inhibition of anti-diuretic hormone. (NB. thyroid function does not change.)

Is human body temperature constant?

The temperature of the resting body varies throughout the day, exhibiting a diurnal or circadian rhythm. It is lowest at night, often falling to 36°C and rises by up to 1.5°C during the day.

Women have a monthly rhythm of temperature and the basal temperature rises by about 0.5°C at ovulation and remains at this high level until the onset of the next menstruation.

25.   MUSCLE CONTRACTION

What is the motor unit?

The motor unit is the basic element of motor control. It consists of an α-motor neuron, its motor axon, and all the skeletal muscle fibres that it innervates. The number of muscle fibres supplied by a single α-motor neuron is determined by the type of movement that the muscle performs, so muscles performing coarse movements (such as quadriceps femoris) will have a large number, and muscles performing fine movements (such as the extraocular muscles) will have a small number.

What is the structure and function of muscle stretch receptors?

Muscle stretch receptors (muscle spindles and golgi tendon organs) are specialised sensory receptors that discharge when the muscle is stretched. They are vital for motor control and proprioception. The most complex is the muscle spindle, which is composed of two types of fibre.

- **Intra-fusal muscle fibres** are richly innervated and enclosed within a connective tissue capsule. They contain two types of fibre: nuclear bag and nuclear chain fibres. The nuclear bag fibres are innervated by large, myelinated group Ia fibres. The nuclear chain fibres are innervated by medium sized, myelinated group II fibres. Gamma motor neurons innervate the intra-fusal muscle fibres to regulate the sensitivity of the muscle spindles to stretch.
- **Extra-fusal fibres** lie between the regular muscle fibres

What is the structure of striated muscle?

- The contractile unit of a striated muscle cell is the sarcomere
- Within one striated muscle cell are large numbers of sarcomeres linked end to end by z disks
- There are two types of sliding muscle filaments, thick and thin. Thick filaments are composed of myosin, consisting of a head projecting from a tail. The head forms the crossbridge to the thin filaments. The thin filaments are composed of actin, tropomyosin and troponin.

What is the mechanism of excitation-contraction coupling?

Muscle cells contract by the sliding filament cross bridge mechanism. There are four steps to this cross bridge mechanism:

1. The ATP bound to myosin is hydrolysed to form a myosin-ADP-phosphate complex with high energy enabling binding to the actin of the thin filament.
2. The ADP and phosphate are released after myosin binds to actin. This causes a confirmational change in the myosin head that results in sliding of the thin fibres towards the centre of the sarcomere (i.e. contraction).

3. The actin-myosin complex binds ATP to release the cross bridge.
4. The myosin ADP-P complex is formed to complete the cycle.

What is the important difference between skeletal and cardiac excitation-contraction coupling?

The important difference is that there is no tetany in cardiac muscle because the action potential is longer than the contractile response.

26.   POTASSIUM HOMEOSTASIS

What is the normal distribution of potassium ions in the body?

Potassium (K^+) is a predominantly intracellular cation with 98% of total body K^+ found inside cells. The normal extracellular concentration of K^+ is between 3.5–5.5 mmol/l.

What are the major mechanisms involved in maintaining K^+ homeostasis?

K^+ homeostasis is primarily maintained by the kidney. The GI tract plays a smaller role. In the kidney, filtered K^+ is almost completely reabsorbed in the proximal tubule. Urinary K^+ excretion is mainly a passive process. However, fine adjustments to K^+ balance are made through active secretion in the distal convoluted tubule. This regulation is under the aldosterone control. Aldosterone stimulates the renal tubular cells to secrete K^+ (and absorb Na^+ concurrently) causing a reduction in plasma K^+.

The amount of K^+ lost in the urine depends on several factors

- The amount of sodium available for reabsorption in the distal convoluted tubule
- The availability of hydrogen and K^+ ions in the cells of the distal convoluted tubule
- The renal tubular fluid flow rate (a decreased flow rate results in a decreased secretion of K^+ and an increase in plasma K^+)

Other endogenous substances have an effect on K^+ levels in the body and they include

- Insulin and adrenaline which cause K^+ to pass from the extracellular fluid into the cells resulting in a reduction in plasma K^+, through its action on the Na^+/K^+ ATPase pump
- ADH also has an effect on K^+ levels

How does acid-base balance affect the distribution of K^+ ions?

- In metabolic acidosis, hydrogen ions are secreted in preference to K^+, thus there is a tendency for K^+ levels to rise. In contrast, in alkalosis, fewer hydrogen ions are available for excretion, therefore more K^+ is excreted.
- Acid-base disturbances due to respiratory disorders have a negligible effect on K^+ homeostasis.

What are the common causes of hypokalaemia in surgical patients?

Can be divided into GI and non GI causes

- **GI causes** include vomiting, diarrhoea, rectal villous adenoma, laxatives, prolonged nasogastric suction and enterocutaneous fistulae
- **Non GI causes** include diuretics (e.g. loop), mineralocorticoid excess, corticosteroid excess, insulin, metabolic alkalosis, inadequate K^+ supplementation

27.   BURNS

What is the fluid replacement regimen for a 70 kg man with 30% burns?

Numerous formulae have been described for fluid replacement. In principle, intravenous fluids are used for burns covering a surface area >10% in children and >15% in adults. Crystalloids containing salt and water are ideal (e.g. 0.9% normal saline containing 0.5 mmol sodium/kg/% burn). The total additional fluid volume is between 2 and 4 ml/kg/ body surface area of burn (%) given over a 36–48 hour period. Salt containing fluid (e.g Dioralyte) (50ml/kg per 24 hrs) is given orally if possible.

The Wallace rule of nines is used to calculate the area of burn.

For the above patient give

*   3500 ml of water orally per 24 hrs
*   IV 0.9% Normal Saline volume of 70 kg x 30% x 3 ml = 6300 ml over 36 hrs (Give 3150 ml over the first 12 hrs)

How do you monitor the fluid replacement?

The fluid replacement is monitored through clinical and haematological assessment.

*   Peripheral circulation
*   Skin colour
*   Pulse rate
*   Blood pressure
*   Hourly urine output measurement
*   Regular haematocrit levels

What are the complications of burns?

*   Mortality from fluid loss and sepsis are the most important complications. The risk increases with age and surface area of burn.
*   Burns with >30% area have increased risk of ARDS, paralytic ileus and stress ulceration (Curling's ulcers)
*   Septicaemia
*   Circumferential burns
*   Myoglobinuria – renal failure
*   Hypovolaemia
*   Hypernatraemia
*   Hyponatraemia
*   Burn diabetes
*   Hypercatabolic states

Which burns will require grafting?

Deep or full thickness burns will not regenerate and therefore are treated by excision and skin grafting. Deep dermal burns may be grafted on the 3rd or 4th post burn day. A less aggressive approach is to assess after two weeks and shave and skin graft unhealed areas.

Superficial burns re-epithelialise rapidly from the remaining basal cells usually with minimal scarring.

Superficial dermal burns also heal by regeneration from undamaged keratinocytes within 10–14 days with little or no scarring. They do not require skin grafting.

28.   THE PITUITARY GLAND

What hormones are secreted from the pituitary?

The **anterior pituitary** (adenohypophysis) secretes

- Growth hormone (GH)
- Prolactin (PRL)
- Thyroid Stimulating hormone (TSH)
- Adrenocorticotrophic hormone (ACTH)
- Follicle Stimulating hormone (FSH)
- Luteinising hormone (LH)

The **posterior pituitary** (neurohypophysis) secretes

- Oxytocin
- Anti-diuretic hormone (ADH)

What are the clinical manifestations of a prolactinoma?

The clinical manifestations typically depend on whether the tumour is a micro (<10 mm in diameter) or macro adenoma (>10 mm in diameter).

The clinical manifestations of a micro prolactinoma are those of hyperprolactinaemia

- Galactorrhoea
- Menstrual irregularities in females
- Infertility in females
- Impotence in males

A macroadenoma usually presents with a mass effect, as it is usually non-secreting. It would therefore cause

- Headache
- Paralysis of the extra-ocular muscles
- Visual field abnormalities (bitemporal hemianopia)
- Anterior pituitary failure (secondary to compression)

What is the medical treatment for hyperprolactinaemia?

In the normal individual, dopamine is secreted from the hypothalamus and inhibits prolactin secretion from the anterior pituitary. Bromocriptine, a dopamine agonist can therefore be used to inhibit prolactin secretion from the anterior pituitary. Bromocriptine is also used to reduce the size of macroadenomas prior to surgery.

What is the difference between Cushing's disease and Cushing's syndrome?

Cushing's syndrome is any clinical condition resulting from excessive, inappropriate exposure to glucocorticoid. It was described by Harvey Cushing in 1932 (the 'father of neurosurgery'). Cushing's disease is where excess glucocorticoid results from a pituitary tumour.

What are the causes of Cushing's syndrome?

- An ACTH secreting pituitary tumour (Cushing's syndrome)
- Steroids
- Ectopic ACTH secretion (oat cell bronchial tumours, gastrointestinal carcinoid tumours, islet cell tumours of the pancreas)
- An adrenal adenoma or carcinoma

What biochemical tests may be useful for elucidating the cause of the Cushing's syndrome?

- **High dose Dexamethasone suppression test.** 2 mg of dexamethasone is given 6 hourly for 48 hours. Plasma cortisol is measured at 0900 on the morning following the last dose. Failure of suppression of cortisol suggests ectopic ACTH production or an adrenal tumour. In Cushing's disease, cortisol decreases to less than 50% of the pre-treatment level.
- **ACTH plasma levels.** Plasma levels are often very high in ectopic secretion and low in adrenal tumours. Cushing's disease produces moderately elevated levels.

The low dose dexamethasone suppression test and 24 hour urinary cortisol excretion levels are only useful as screening tests.

29. MICTURITION

Can you briefly describe to me the structure of the bladder?

The bladder may be anatomically described in two parts – the **trigone** and the **fundus**. The trigone is a relatively fixed triangular base of the bladder the apex of which forms the posterior lip at the bladder neck at the internal urethral meatus. One of the ureters enters the bladder at the upper two angles. The trigone is supported by stout fibro-muscular ligaments which extend from the inferior aspect of the pubic bones in the region of the bladder neck. There are pubo-prostatic ligaments in the male and pubo-urethral ligaments in the female which aid fixation of the trigone and maintain the position of the bladder as the fundus expands and contracts.

The **fundus** of the bladder consists of three layers, an outer adventitial, a middle muscular and an inner mucosal layer. The adventitial layer is mainly composed of loose connective tissue, whilst the bladder mucosa is of the transitional type of epithelium. The smooth muscle of the bladder, called the detrusor and is the principle component of the bladder wall.

Can you briefly describe the initiation and control of voiding?

Once the threshold of filling has been reached in the bladder, there is increased afferent activity which reaches conscious level and one becomes aware that the bladder is filling. The spinal cord integrates this afferent information from the bladder and also receives afferent inputs from the pelvic, hypogastric and lumbar nerves which run to the brain stem.

The centres responsible for the co-ordination of micturition lie in the brain stem. Impulses that facilitate the micturition reflex are thought to originate in the 'pontine micturition centre'. There is a complex series of reflexes which involve many areas of the brain with inputs to the 'brain stem micturition centre'. There are **major descending pathways** that lead from the brain stem and converge on the 'sacral micturition centre', which is a group of cells lying in the grey matter (Onuf's nucleus) in the ventral horn of the sacral spinal cord (S2). These cell bodies are the motor neurones which supply the external urethral sphincter.

The **cerebral cortex** is important in the control of micturition having an overall inhibitory effect on the detrusor muscle.

What is the innervation of the detrusor muscle?

The detrusor muscle receives parasympathetic innervation via the pelvic nerves (S2–S4) and is responsible for bladder contraction. In addition, it receives a sympathetic innervation via the hypogastric nerves T10–L2 which produces detrusor relaxation.

How does the bladder store urine?

The bladder is able to store urine because it possesses intrinsic tone and exhibits receptive relaxation i.e. the vesical lumen can expand without a concomitant rise in intra-vesical pressure. These viscoelastic properties of the bladder and intrinsic ability of the muscle to retain a constant tension over a wide range of stretch allow the bladder to store urine. The other major factor controlling bladder storage is neural inhibitory control.

30.   BRAIN STEM DEATH

What are the preconditions for diagnosing brain stem death?

- The patient is in an apnoeic coma (the patient is maintained on a ventilator because spontaneous respiration has previously become inadequate or ceased)
- There is demonstrable, structural and irreversible brain damage due to a disorder that can cause brain stem death which has been diagnosed with certainty

What conditions may mimic brain stem death and therefore should be excluded before making such a diagnosis?

- Sedative drugs, alcohol, poisons or neuromuscular blocking agents
- Primary hypothermia
- Metabolic or endocrine disturbances

What tests are used to diagnose brain stem death?

One must establish that all brain stem reflexes are absent.

- The pupils are fixed in diameter and unresponsive to bright light
- Absent corneal reflexes
- Absent vestibulo-ocular reflexes (caloric test)
- Absent oculocephalic reflexes
- No motor responses within the cranial nerve distribution to painful stimuli applied centrally or peripherally
- No gag or cough reflexes in response to pharyngeal, laryngeal or tracheal stimulation
- No spontaneous respiratory movements when the patient is ventilated with 5% carbon dioxide and 95% oxygen for 10 minutes and then disconnected from the ventilator for a further 10 minutes. A blood gas sample is taken to ensure that the arterial carbon dioxide tension is >6.7 kPa.

Is there a role for EEG?

In the UK, it is not necessary to perform EEG as a confirmatory test as it is though to be misleading.

Who should carry out the examination?

Two doctors are required to perform the examination for brain stem death. One of the doctors should be the consultant in charge of the case and the other clinician should be of at least 5 years post registration. Neither should be a member of the transplant team.

When should the test be carried out?

The test should only be performed a minimum of 6 hours after the onset of the coma or 24 hours post cardiac arrest.

Index